Don't Take My Word for It
But, don't take theirs either

How to avoid "Buying the Can" from someone else; learning what God has in mind.

Revised First Edition
by
Keith T Jenkins

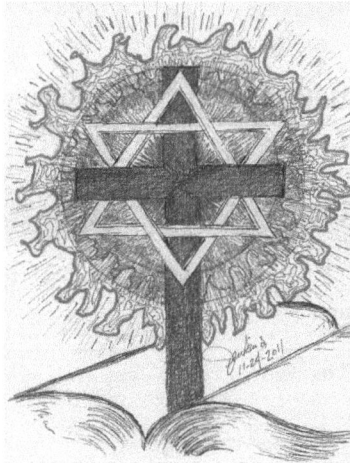

Keith T Jenkins Family Publishers
San Antonio, Texas

Edited by Patricia A Jenkins

With help from friends:
Kelly Morris – William Grace – Cynthia Lopez
&
Jessica Garcia

A Reminder:

Multiplied - by NeedToBreathe
www.needtobreathe.com

Your love is
      Like radiant diamonds
Bursting inside us
      We cannot contain
Your love will
      Surely come find us
Like blazing wildfires
      Singing your name

God of mercy
      Sweet love of mine
I have surrendered to your design
      May this offering stretch across the sky
        And these hallelujahs be multiplied.

Cross & Hammer Publishing
354 Consuelo Av
San Antonio, Texas 78228

https://www.facebook.com/CrossAndHammerPublishing

Please note that there are places in Scripture passages where the grammar or punctuation may be contrary to current application, and where it's past, present and future tense may be in conflict, but that is because the Scriptures were copied from their electronic source directly, without editing at all on the part of the author in any way, so as to preserve the original content of the Scripture, and to never stand accused of editing the Word in any way.

Published by Cross & Hammer Publishing April, 2015

Table of Contents

Introduction

The first thing you should know is that I believe in an awesome God, the same from the beginning of time, powerful beyond measure. And, I believe in miracles. Let me tell you part of the reason why.

There was a boy who, when he was about two took a rather large fall from a retaining wall to a drive way, about six feet below, and the cement met his head with an unforgiving force. The boy's skull was fractured about eighty percent of the way around, and he received what was termed "acquired epilepsy." At that point things went terribly wrong. The parents spent a lot of time in and out of hospitals, and weeks would go by with the home having one parent, or a sitter, and the other parent at the hospital, and sometimes both. The parents prayed constantly.

The boy would come home. The boy would go back. He would get momentarily better, and then monumentally worse. He was having as many as twenty five grand-mal seizures a day. Sometimes his brother would have to sit on him and grab his ears to hold him as still as possible so that he did not bash his head open on the floor. The mother tells of how she had been praying for what seemed a lifetime, "God, please save my son." The father, being a military man, of authority and under authority – we have all heard the Centurion's story (Matthew 8:5-13) – had surrendered long ago and was praying constantly for grace to cope.

The situation had gotten desperate and the boy had taken a severe turn for the worse and was spiraling downward on a steady path. One particular day, when the parents went to confer with his doctor, they were told, "We need to start thinking about where your son is going to finish out his final days. We can't help him anymore."

That night the mom and dad went home and the prayers changed. Resignation had set in, perspectives had been altered, and that night the mother prayed, "He is not my child but yours, God. There is nothing I can do about any of it, except to ask for your strength to handle whatever you decide to do." She had finally surrendered ownership of the boy. She wasn't making any more decisions and she wasn't taking any more authority in the matter. She had given up . . . let go.

The next morning, the couple went to the hospital with their resignations to learn about what kind of facilities would be available for the boy, and they found the place was abuzz with nurses scurrying about in a frantic opus of joy. One of the nurses stopped to speak to the bewildered parents and said, "We don't know what's happening, and we have several tests yet to do, but it looks like your son is completely well! It looks like he doesn't have epilepsy anymore." The parents were almost apoplectic with joy, and I haven't had a seizure since.

As Paul would say, I am an "unprofitable servant" with a checkered past, and, like Paul, I have a very high I.Q. and a willingness to use it, especially on the Scriptures, without a desire to run away from them and what they say. I grew up in a military family with an officer for a dad, who was the primary bread winner, and a mom who usually participated in and often led the Officer's Wives Club. In the

1

sixties she sold vacuum cleaners or cosmetics to make Christmas money or vacation funds, but never really needed a job outside the house, and let's face it, the kids were enough.

I am the middle of three kids with an older brother and younger sister, and among my earliest memories, a cousin named Geri lived with us until she got married when I was about 3 or 4, I think. My brother, Bruce (six years my senior), was my mom's from a previous marriage when she was seventeen, and I did not know about that until I was about fifteen. My father had adopted him and never mentioned it or treated him any differently, as far as I could tell. My sister, Julie, was "Miss Perfect," worked hard, made great grades, played tennis (Dad's athletic passion), at a near professional level, and was my father's pride and joy. I was the damaged one. I was the rebellious kid with the long hair and loud music. I was a Rock and Roll drummer. I got the bad grades and paid little attention in class, helped my older brother sometimes with his homework, but rarely did my own. I did everything wrong. And even though I did it all wrong, I occasionally did it well, or well enough to get by. As you can see, there were plenty of reasons for me to be screwed up; and I was for a long time. Who knows, maybe I still am. You decide.

My mom would later say that, because she and my brother, spent the early years depending only upon themselves, that they had a "special bond" like no other. But the way in which manifested itself as regards the family structure was me being the second best son. She let me know that I was "learning disabled" but never told me how. Three decades would pass before I knew that I was an ADD kid. And by not telling me, she left me believing that it was something horrendous. After all, I was damaged.

Growing up in a military family meant that my parent's disappointment in me was usually more a matter of how it reflected on Dad's rank and position than just disappointment in me personally. I remember that when my parents discovered that I had a sex life I was in trouble, not because my girlfriend and I were having sex, but because of with whom I had sex (she was the daughter of a Warrant Officer and my dad was a Colonel), and where, and who knew about it, and how they found out about it. It was a near public scandal that, although not rank threatening, doubtless cost him some respect among the troops, most of whom were under his command.

One of the greatest benefits of being an army brat was that I would go to seventeen schools before I got to a college, and that I probably had real and intimate conversations with nearly ten thousand adults before I became one. This gave me a very real advantage when it came to reasoning things out, finding truth, and understanding realities of life.

When we were in Kansas (last half of my first 6th Grade year) my dad and I had a lot more time together without the military world. We worked livestock together, visited neighbors who were not military, and shared a lot of thoughts. It was there that my dad first told me that if he had a choice, he would have been a Jew. Little did he know . . .?

I mentioned "my first 6th Grade year" because I did have a second. My grades were not failing, but not great either, and I was small for my age. My

2

mother insists that the reason I was held back that year was the matter of my size, maybe – she would occasionally relent – also my maturity, but looking back; I don't know.

Strangely, when my dad was assigned to the Pentagon, he was the busiest ever, leaving in the dark of morning, coming home in the dark of evening; but when he was off, he was done. We would sometimes go to Solomon's Island on Chesapeake Bay and fish all day. We would leave before dawn, come back well into the night, and go to church in the morning. These were the best days of my youth. During these times, my father built into me the idea of trying to fully think a matter through, not stopping when it was convenient or when the answer that you wanted first appeared, but later in my life that would not always be what happened.

Spiritually, I grew up in a Lutheran household. My parents were involved in planting several new Lutheran congregations in my childhood, the last being Prince of Peace Lutheran in east San Antonio in the late sixties. We were ALC in one town, and LCA in another, Missouri Synod in Kansas, and ELCA in the end. I did Sunday School and Catechism, was confirmed, and then got saved in a Baptist tent meeting when I was almost twenty, where I accepted Jesus as Savior. It would be about another decade or more before He would become Lord to me.

In the meantime I went to the "Protestant" services on post, sang in a Catholic choir for their services, dated a Mormon girl for about a week, went to a Methodist church for about a year, I attended Episcopal services for a while and more. We have been associated with Pentecostals, Mennonites, and Evangelical Free churches, as well as non-denominational, and even anti-denominational organizations. I first started seriously digging into the Word at a Presbyterian Bible study, which was (I would later learn) rather liberal in thought, and in 1995 I graduated from International Bible College, a conservative and independent Pentecostal place of learning founded by an amazing missionary to Japan, named Leonard Coote. He had returned home to the US during WWII and founded the school, just as he had the Ikoma Bible College in Japan. I completed their two year program, which had previously been an Associates program.

It was at IBC that I learned to try my best to take the Bible as it is, instead of as someone else may say it is. At IBC I was given access to a collection of tools and the training to use them without having to use them in the way someone else said to. I was not doing Pentecostal Bible Study, or Catholic Bible Study, or anyone else's predefined version of theology but learning to find in the Bible what was is in the Bible and nothing more, but also nothing less. And, to some degree, it has been my resurrection, and my undoing.

Since I have been to school and seen how the tools are available, the learning is available for anyone, and most of it costs so very little, I get terribly annoyed with pastors and preachers and teachers that mishandle the Scriptures. I don't mean minor errors and omissions, but glazing over blatant parts of the text that disagree with the idea that is being proposed or the point that is being made. This is the core of the reason for the book, and most of my life in the Church anymore.

On two occasions I saw different pastors, of different faith families, dealing faithlessly with Jesus in Nazareth speaking in a synagogue and later they tried to kill him. Here is the text:

> Luke 4:16-29 (NASB) And He came to Nazareth, where He had been brought up; and as was His custom, He entered the synagogue on the Sabbath, and stood up to read. And the book of the prophet Isaiah was handed to Him. And He opened the book and found the place where it was written, "The Spirit of the Lord is upon Me, because He anointed Me to preach the gospel to the poor. He has sent Me to proclaim release to the captives, and recovery of sight to the blind, to set free those who are oppressed, to proclaim the favorable year of the Lord."
>
> And He closed the book, gave it back to the attendant and sat down; and the eyes of all in the synagogue were fixed on Him.
>
> And He began to say to them, "Today this Scripture has been fulfilled in your hearing."
>
> And all were speaking well of Him, and wondering at the gracious words which were falling from His lips; and they were saying, "Is this not Joseph's son?"
>
> And He said to them, "No doubt you will quote this proverb to Me, 'Physician, heal yourself! Whatever we heard was done at Capernaum, do here in your hometown as well.' "
>
> And He said, "Truly I say to you, no prophet is welcome in his hometown. But I say to you in truth, there were many widows in Israel in the days of Elijah, when the sky was shut up for three years and six months, when a great famine came over all the land; and yet Elijah was sent to none of them, but only to Zarephath, in the land of Sidon, to a woman who was a widow. And there were many lepers in Israel in the time of Elisha the prophet; and none of them was cleansed, but only Naaman the Syrian."
>
> And all the people in the synagogue were filled with rage as they heard these things; and they got up and drove Him out of the city, and led Him to the brow of the hill on which their city had been built, in order to throw Him down the cliff.

On both occasions of which I speak, each of the pastors were adamant that when Jesus told the people that He was Messiah, "Today this Scripture has been fulfilled in your hearing," the congregation got angry and tried to kill him.

But this is not the case. After He told them that He was the Expected One "all were speaking well of Him, and wondering at the gracious words which were falling from His lips." It was not until He told them that He would not be doing his "dog and pony show" that they got angry. After He told them that the prophet is not welcome in his hometown and that God often has to reveal His power to outsiders and elsewhere – THAT is when the congregation got angry.

In both cases, with both pastors, I addressed this error, and both of them said that they had gotten it correctly and that I misunderstood the passage. According to them, even after reviewing the text, seeing the context, to them, Jesus announced that he was Messiah and the crowd immediately became rabid. I want better for you. If you are reading this book, I expect better of you. Please strive and succeed.

In the KJV, Paul says to Timothy (2 Timothy 2:15) "Study to shew thyself approved unto God, a workman that needeth not to be ashamed, rightly dividing the word of truth." In the NIV it reads, "Do your best to present yourself to God as one approved, a workman who does not need to be ashamed and who correctly handles the word of truth." The NASB gives it as, "Be diligent to present yourself approved to God as a workman who does not need to be ashamed, accurately handling the word of truth." But whether you are "rightly dividing" it, or if you correctly and accurately handle it, remember that it is the Word of Truth. You should "study" and "do your best" and be tirelessly "diligent" in the pursuit of Scripture, because Scripture deserves it. The Scriptures deserve the most careful and honest translating, reading, interpretation, and application of all texts we could ever handle, because they are the most powerful that people we share them with will ever receive. Please, do so. Please be careful and diligent and share the Word with someone who will receive it . . . fully, honestly, carefully. Look at the choice they offer.

> Deuteronomy 30:15-20 (NIV) See, I set before you today life and prosperity, death and destruction. For I command you today to love the Lord your God, to walk in his ways, and to keep his commands, decrees and laws; then you will live and increase, and the Lord your God will bless you in the land you are entering to possess. But if your heart turns away and you are not obedient, and if you are drawn away to bow down to other gods and worship them, I declare to you this day that you will certainly be destroyed. You will not live long in the land you are crossing the Jordan to enter and possess. This day I call heaven and earth as witnesses against you that I have set before you life and death, blessings and curses. Now choose life, so that you and your children may live and that you may love the Lord your God, listen to his voice, and hold fast to him. For the Lord is your life, and he will give you many years in the land he swore to give to your fathers, Abraham, Isaac and Jacob.

> Choose life, please, and share it with someone else.

> In Deuteronomy 6:6ff we read:

These commandments that I give you today are to be on your hearts. Impress them on your children. Talk about them when you sit at home and when you walk along the road, when you lie down and when you get up. Tie them as symbols on your hands and bind them on your foreheads. Write them on the doorframes of your houses and on your gates.

The importance of the Scriptures is such that God wants them to "be on your hearts" and share them with our kids. They are to be a part of what we are and make them a part of our children as well. Scripture is to be a part of our daily conversation, in our rising and lying down and all along the way. When He said to bind them to our hands He wants us to have our work reflect His word, and whatever you do with your hands should remind you of Him. When He tells us to place the word on our foreheads, He wants it to be between what we see and what we think. Scripture should be the filter through which we view the world. And when we put them on our doorposts and gates, Scriptures become the filter by which the World views us.

Is there a fish on your windshield? Is there a mezuzah at your door? Is there a Cross at the gate to your land? Does the world know that you are His?

My Hero Martin

The most important thing to remember about Martin Luther is, not that he was a hero of mine, which he was, but that he was a teacher of theology at a small town university. His qualifications were that he held a Bachelor's degree in Biblical studies, and another in "Sentences" – followed by a Doctorate of Theology and having been called to Wittenberg in the position of "Doctor in Bible." Now, these may sound like magnificent titles, but in reality we must recall that these degrees were conferred by a theological organization that is known for its imaginative application of Scripture, and in the case of the Apocrypha, the invention and spurious designation of Scripture for the purpose of generating support for special elements of otherwise, non-biblical theology. In fact, it took him four years from entry at the University of Erfurt, which he later described as a "beerhouse and whorehouse," to receive his Masters through what he called, "days of rote learning, and often wearying spiritual exercises." As far as actual theology is concerned, the Catholic Corporation of the day, would rather that no one actually DO theology, only recite and repeat it. The evidence of this is in the lives and deaths of myriad martyrs along the way a couple hundred years before and after Luther. Jan Hus (John Hus or John Huss) was among them about a hundred years before Luther, and was put to death by burning at the stake, by the church, and his last words are said to have been, "God is my witness that the things charged against me I never preached. In the same truth of the Gospel which I have written, taught, and preached, drawing upon the sayings and positions of the holy

6

doctors, I am ready to die today." Hus had preached pretty much the same stuff as Luther, and since they could find no actual and theological fault in his teachings, he was killed for their inconvenience and found guilty on imaginary charges.

On October 31, 1517 Martin Luther (formerly Hans Luder) did several things. He got out of bed and had breakfast, he sent a letter to his bishop and enclosed a copy of "Disputation of Martin Luther on the Power and Efficacy of Indulgences," and then nailed a copy of it on the door of the church at Wittenberg, Germany. This "Disputation" came to be known as the "Ninety Five Theses," and in it Martin purposed a discussion on any or all of the topics it contained. A student or a teacher could post some thesis or theses for public appraisal and then later, someone would be chosen to pick a side and debate the matters. It was intended as a scholarly exercise and an opportunity for some lively local debate, a fairly common form of entertainment at the time; since they did not have television and YouTube. And because there were no "news" agencies, this could also be a means by which information was disseminated among the academics and aristocracy as well as the peasants. Besides, when two learned men of the Word would discuss and debate its particulars and merits, the locals would receive far more from it than if it were presented in a sermon. What started as an invitation to scholarly debate, partly for entertainment and partly for the informing of the students at the university there, ended up being a world changing launching pad, not unlike the "shot heard round the world."

In the end, Luther was excommunicated and branded an outlaw and many times, Rome tried to have him killed. Those who read the theses today find them more searching and inquisitive rather than insulting or accusatory. Although, there were some that were more pointed than others, like thesis 86 asking, "Why does the pope, whose wealth today is greater than the wealth of the richest Crassus, build the basilica of St. Peter with the money of poor believers rather than with his own money?"

One friend and colleague of Luther, Johannes Agricola, whose name means "John the Farmer" wrote about brother Martin's posting of the theses, "certain theses in the year of 1517 according to the customs of University of Wittenberg as part of a scientific discussion. The presentation of the theses was done in a modest and respectful way, preventing to mock or insult anybody." So, witnesses of the day, which were not of the Catholic hierarchy and were not profiting from indulgences, found no offense in the work. And in this work, I join Martin Luther, as a fellow explorer of the Scriptures and seeker of Truth.

Now, I realize that there are many people out there who will shout, "How dare you compare yourself to Martin Luther!" And that's okay. I want each of us to compare ourselves to Martin Luther. I want people to realize that, like everyone that will read this book, I have Luther and Hus to rely upon for past reflection, as well as Barth, Bonheoffer, and more. I did not grow up and stay to study in the shadow of a corrupt organization, but instead, had available to me some of the finest tools for Scripture Mining that have ever been discovered or invented, along with several hundred years of archeology. And, unlike Luther and Hus, I was born again before I started digging, and had excellent translations available in my native tongue, and I have the willingness to be found wrong by the Scriptures, my peers, and by my God.

Just as a note: Archeology was originated by its "founder" Flavio Biondo and the "father of archaeology" Ciriaco de' Pizzicolli, "humanists" to the core and at the heart of their studies, scriblings, and teachings were the ideas, the driving desire, to prove the Bible historically and culturally wrong.

One of the great instigators for disavowing of the Bible by many victims of the "Enlightenment" was the idea that there were no signs of Nineveh, which figures so prominently in the Biblical record. Another was that no one would behave as Abraham did by taking his wife's servant to bed to spawn an heir. But it was Archeology that has since proven the Biblical record time and time again, and even Nineveh was found three hundred years after Luther's life. And the cities of Byblos and Nuzi were discovered to contain countless contracts and records of births of heirs, called "the child of my lap" by the adoptive mother – married to the father who would conceive – usually by his wife's servant, or a servant purchased for her, for this purpose.

Remember that Luther started out in his quest as a storm-scared man who became a monk, devoutly following in the traditions, training, and philosophy of the organization that would later disown him for disagreeing with their tainted version of the Gospel. Considering how much the "organization" had bent the truth with each succeeding generation after the cross, is it amazing at all that Mohammed could invent and sell the plan of Islam?

If we are to accurately and deftly combat Islam, and all the other anti-Christian or pseudo-Christian cults that are snagging our weak and untrained, we will have to be diligent, honest, thorough, and plain. And make no mistake, there is combat to be waged in these matters. I believe that one of the things we need is a new "Ninety Five." In the Sixteenth Century, when Martin posed queries about accepted theological practices he was confronted by the force of all that was Rome, and when his continued existence came into question, his reply to the demand that he recant was,

> "Unless I am convinced by the testimony of the Scriptures or by clear reason (for I do not trust either in the pope or in councils alone, since it is well known that they have often erred and contradicted themselves), I am bound by the Scriptures I have quoted and my conscience is captive to the Word of God. I cannot and will not recant anything, since it is neither safe nor right to go against conscience. May God help me. Amen."

The same is true about all the things we believe that are not of Scripture. We must be convinced by Scripture and clear reason (sound reason) on everything. Brother Martin gave this summation at the conclusion of the examination of his writings at the Diet of Worms from 28 January to 25 May 1521, with Emperor Charles V presiding.

It is essential that we rely upon clear reason (sound reason), what some translate as "plain reason," when dealing with the Scriptures because we can apply enough "wisdom not from above" to allow for the text to be convoluted into saying exactly the opposite of what it plainly says. This is especially common when dealing with Law, but I will seek to more reasonably address that matter later on. My point is that we should be careful to not twist the words of the text to fit the will of our own hearts.

Chapter 1 – So What?

When I was at International Bible College in San Antonio, Texas, a professor named Van Gill walked into the classroom on our first day of "Pentateuch" and wrote two simple words on the chalkboard. Then he came around and sat down on the front edge of the desk and began. The two words he wrote were, "SO WHAT!"

The words he then spoke went something like this; "So what?" he asked. "What does it matter how we understand the creation story? Who cares who Cain's wife was? So what difference does it make how we read the 'Sons of God and Daughters of Men?' How could it really matter how we apply sexual purity laws or the Beatitudes? So what, if Paul says that '*all scripture* is God-Breathed,' and if Jesus tells us that 'Man does not live by bread alone but by *every word* that proceeds from the mouth of God?' So what?"

In that moment a light came on in my head and I realized that the important parts of Scripture are not the ones that I feel are important. Instead, the important parts are the ones that God felt important enough to make Scripture. Once I got away from using the "Hunt and Peck" method of theology it became easier to do theology, and simultaneously much more difficult. It also became easier to see, and some day, strive to become what God wants me to be and to do what He wants me to do. It is more like mining, and the Scriptures are the Gold – and the rest of the reading material of the world is silver, lead, copper, iron, dross and refuse. And much of it is far worse than "wood, hay and stubble."

Another thing that made a difference was in realizing that God had left the Bible behind for me to find, not as a guide book full of good ideas and suggestions, and not as an Owner's Manual, but – in computer terms – it was a User's Manual with an End User License Agreement. Just like the fact that you don't OWN the software that you buy, but only hold a license to use it, you don't OWN your life. But you are born with a "squatter's right" to use it, and you are given a license from the true owner of the item, and the rightful owner of that life is God.

The importance of Scripture Mining is to use it to find what is true about everything we can, and to put that Truth to use as best we can. And, in order to avoid any pitfalls from the past, we must refuse to do what I call, "Buying the Can." Buying the Can means to take whatever is handed to us (theologically, philosophically, politically, romantically, economically, etc.) and simply assume that it is correct. After all, all of those men who did all that study to get all those answers In the Can for you must have done a good job. Right? They must have, at least, done a better job than you and I could do. Right? Maybe not.

Every religious organization has done extensive "study" to come up with a point of view that is uniquely their own, but still, views vary. Then we have to accept that if they are too unique they may not be Christian. There should be some elements that are "uniquely" Christian, and therefore, held as true by all Christian organizations.

The Biblical Christian point of view is that Jesus is the Eternal God in person, while Jehovah's Witnesses claim that he is actually the Archangel Michael. Mormons believe that Jesus is the son of the god of *this planet*, who is actually Adam (also called Elohim) and that Adam had intercourse with Eve (his primary Celestial Wife) to create all people on this world and then had intercourse with another wife, Mary, to bring Jesus into the world. Jesus, with Adam's other son, Lucifer, would struggle together to bring all mankind to the knowledge of the truth from knowledge of Good and Evil.

Muslims believe that Jesus was a prophet who never actually died, as the crucifixion account claims, but instead was taken live into heaven as a special favor, like that bestowed upon Enoch in the book of Genesis. But, given the divergence of those ideas, no two of them can be true at the same time. Life is not "Star Wars[1]." Jesus is not Obi Wan Kenobi. And what is "truth" does not actually depend on your certain point of view.

If you believe that Jesus is the Eternal God and that He has died for your sins to save you from the pit of hell, and that everyone needs Salvation, what do you have to back up your theology? Did you just get this from someone at a bus stop one day and that was the end of the investigation? That is how a thousand people will become Muslim, Mormons, or Jehovah's Witnesses this month. Someone will tell them something in a plausible sounding way and they will "Buy the Can." And in Buying the Can they will also buy a ticket straight to Hell, unless someone else can get them to believe something else, and they can't very well do that without something to back up their words. And that is where a fuller knowledge of Scripture is indispensable. And you've got to start somewhere;

> Romans 10:14-15 (NIV) How, then, can they call on the one they have not believed in? And how can they believe in the one of whom they have not heard? And how can they hear without someone preaching to them? And how can they preach unless they are sent? As it is written, "How beautiful are the feet of those who bring good news!"

I was in a conversation with a Lutheran Intern – Pastorette in Training – and she was upset, saying, "Left up to you, people would be frightened into the Kingdom of God!" To which I replied, "Lady, I would be willing to take them at gun-point if I thought it would work." Now, that is a bit out of context, and I know that evangelism at gun-point won't work, but the point is this – people won't get into the Kingdom if we don't do something. She had said that she was sure that God had a plan for people to get into Heaven without us having to do anything to help them become Christians and that there would be Muslims and Buddhists and Hindi there. So, I asked her why, and she replied, "Based on John 3:16," which she then recited. When I asked if she had read verses seventeen and eighteen; she had the strangest "deer in the headlights" look on her face. She said, "I don't know what you mean." So, I opened my Bible and showed her. She was dumbstruck to see that Jesus did not come to condemn the world, but that it was condemned already – for not believing in Him. So, how do we change that? How do we get them to believe in Him? Someone has to say *something*!

The difference between this EULA (End User License Agreement) and those in the computer world is this: In the computer world, if you do not accept the EULA, the software will not install, and in the computer world, you can click that you accept the agreement without ever having read or considered what it says, and most do exactly that.

The EULA

In God's Kingdom you get to continue going through life trying to run the show entirely on your own strengths as long as you will. Even as a Christian you can do this. Also, you don't have to read the whole license agreement to enter into the agreement – someone can give you a "nutshell version" and you agree – without ever having picked up the document yourself. But, you cannot just click the "Agree" button and enter the Kingdom, or maybe just think that you have entered the Kingdom. Let me explain.

How could someone click the "Agree" button in this case? Simple, they go to church and act like a wonderful person. In some cases, they go to church all their lives, even after their parents quit taking them. They may go to Sunday Services because they feel it helps make them a better person, and they may do Sonday School because they get more direct training in how to live that "Christian Life." But are they actually Christians? Who knows?

BTW, Sonday is the day we Worship the Son.

When I was a child (ten or so), I thought it would probably be great to be a Pastor. After all, he drove a pretty nice car, lived in a fine house, really worked only two days a week, had dinner at everyone else's houses, was appreciated for being an all around great guy, and when he talked, people listened. Of course, thinking about it like that, in that simple and childlike way, it looks like a great job, and I can see why there are so many unsaved pastors in the world. But, for the same reasons, there are millions of people that have clicked "Agree." Problem is that when their end of days has come and they stand before the Throne of God, having clicked "Agree" will not cut it. They will be asked why they should be allowed into the Kingdom of God, and if they have the wrong answer . . . well, damn!

Please understand that I don't for a moment believe that you and I have to have the same identical theology for you to get into Eternal Rest and enjoy the Grace of God. There are plenty of articles of faith about which we could argue vehemently and both still arrive in Heaven. But, there are some things that are not up for debate. We can debate the Sons of God and Daughters of Men, angels watching out for women with short hair and even the Creation of the Universe and the Religion of Evolution and the philosophical foolishness of Christians voting Democrat. But when we come down to the subject of how to enter the Kingdom, we had better be right, because straight is the path and narrow the way. So, I am thinking that correct choices and valid options are limited.

"I tell you the truth, the man who does not enter the sheep pen by the gate, but climbs in by some other way, is a thief and a robber. The man who enters by the gate is the shepherd of his sheep." (John 10:1-2 NIV) In this passage, and the words that follow, Jesus describes himself, as opposed to all others who presume to find another way into the Kingdom – what they are, what they do and where they will lead their followers.

In his speech to the Elders of Ephesus, Paul said,

> Acts 20:28-31 NIV "Keep watch over yourselves and all the flock of which the Holy Spirit has made you overseers. Be shepherds of the church of God, which he bought with his own blood. I know that after I leave, savage wolves will come in among you and will not spare the flock. Even from your own number men will arise and distort the truth in order to draw away disciples after them. So be on your guard! Remember that for three years I never stopped warning each of you night and day with tears."

Look closely at that statement, "Even from your own number," and realize that Paul was foreseeing that there would be false leaders, immediately, and these false teachers would spring up from among men who studied with Paul and the first generation ministry team.

Paul was adamant enough about his contemporaries, and eventually us, getting it right that he wrote:

> Galatians 1:6-9 NIV "I am astonished that you are so quickly deserting the one who called you by the grace of Christ and are turning to a different gospel – which is really no gospel at all. Evidently some people are throwing you into confusion and are trying to pervert the gospel of Christ. But even if we or an angel from heaven should preach a gospel other than the one we preached to you, let him be eternally condemned! As we have already said, so now I say again: If anybody is preaching to you a gospel other than what you accepted, let him be eternally condemned!"

It is evident that Jesus and Paul – and all the rest of them for that matter – want us all to get it right, or as right as we can. After all, Luke 11:52 (NASB) "Woe to you lawyers (students of the Law)! For you have taken away the key of knowledge; you yourselves did not enter, and you hindered those who were entering." Could not this be just as easily said to myriad Bible teachers, church leaders, and popes over the centuries since? The answer is an emphatic, "Yes!" And still, don't forget, "For God so loved the world that he gave his one and only Son, that whoever believes in him shall not perish but have eternal life."

13

Remember that God loves us and wants us to get it right, and that men will lead us astray – in fact, just as Jesus said to the lawyers above, men will even lead themselves astray. So, be careful. I don't want you to take my word for any of this, but don't take theirs either. Take the Word of God and learn to dig into it in order to find the Truth of God, and use that Truth to access the Eternal Kingdom that God has waiting for you – not just after death, but Today!

Here is my take on it. I am going to try to put it into language that is simple because, as I see it, the message is simple. If it were not simple enough, only intelligent people could enter Heaven, and that does not really seem like a very Godly idea. So, here goes.

1. I am a dirt bag sinner worthy of death and Hell, and so are you. I brought it on myself and have no one else to blame. (Romans 3:23 NIV) "For all have sinned and fall short of the glory of God."

2. My sin and yours will lead each of us into the Eternal Prison of Hell – the "second death." (Romans 6:23 NIV) "For the wages of sin is death, but the gift of God is eternal life in Christ Jesus our Lord."

3. Even though we are guilty and dirty, Jesus gave his life to save us. (Romans 5:8 NIV) "But God demonstrates his own love for us in this: While we were still sinners, Christ died for us."

4. Finally, if we truly believe Jesus' payment of death on the cross was for our sin – yours and mine – and give our lives over to Him as master, we will be saved. (Romans 10:9-10 NIV) "That if you confess with your mouth, 'Jesus is Lord,' and believe in your heart that God raised him from the dead, you will be saved. For it is with your heart that you believe and are justified, and it is with your mouth that you confess and are saved."

Now, this is the nutshell version, commonly called the "Roman Road," and it is considered by much of Christianity as the real meat of the matter. It is simple and powerful, but it is also easily deniable. It is easy to say that there is more to the Christian faith than this – or less. But saying it is so doesn't make it a fact, or I could "say" that I can fly, and I would be off to Tahiti. But things just don't work that way, do they?

Still, it is the way of men to try to find a way to dismiss God's rule in things and have their own way. Cain did it in wanting to bring what he decided was an acceptable offering, instead of doing what Abel did, and bringing what was required. In Psalms we see:

Psalm 2:1-3 (NIV)
Why do the nations conspire
    And the peoples plot in vain?

14

> The kings of the earth take their stand
> > And the rulers gather together
> > Against the Lord and against his Anointed One (*Messiah*).
> "Let us break their chains," they say,
> > "And throw off their fetters."

And to combat the nature of all people to rebel, there is a promise and (Acts 2:39 NIV) "the promise is for you and your children and for all who are far off – for all whom the Lord our God will call." It is for you and me to reach out and take hold. That promise is Salvation and Resurrection. So, take hold.

At this point I want to express the most significant purpose of this writing, and that is to make people think. I want people to be Saved by coming to the true knowledge of Christ Jesus, the Messiah of God, but also, to consider all the other things that He has for us in the Scriptures. If we only accept Salvation and nothing more, we are as Paul says, just living off the Milk (I Cor. 3:2) and not growing into the meat-eating soldiers of the Lord we are meant to be. As Paul says to Jewish followers;

> Hebrews 5:11-14 (NIV) We have much to say about this, but it is hard to explain because you are slow to learn. In fact, though by this time you ought to be teachers, you need someone to teach you the elementary truths of God's word all over again. You need milk, not solid food! Anyone who lives on milk, being still an infant, is not acquainted with the teaching about righteousness. But solid food is for the mature, who by constant use have trained themselves to distinguish good from evil.

Later Paul said, in Ephesians 4:14 (NASB) "As a result, we are no longer to be children, tossed here and there by waves and carried about by every wind of doctrine, by the trickery of men, by craftiness in deceitful scheming," or as we may say in modern vernacular, "Grow up! Don't be such a child!"

And that is the bottom line; is it not? After being saved, to grow up and learn to distinguish Good from Evil in all things, and to choose the Good. In this way Orthodoxy leads to Orthopraxy. Right Knowledge leads to Right Actions. So, let's see what we can do.

> Deuteronomy 30:19-20 (NASB) "I call heaven and earth to witness against you today, that I have set before you life and death, the blessing and the curse. So choose life in order that you may live, you and your descendants, by loving the Lord your God, by obeying His voice, and by holding fast to Him; for this is your life and the length of your days, that you may live in the land which the Lord swore to your fathers, to Abraham, Isaac, and Jacob, to give them."

In the reverse of the second Psalm, I offer the second to last Psalm:

Psalm 149:1-9 (NIV)

Praise the Lord. Sing to the Lord a new song, his praise in
          the assembly of the saints.
Let Israel rejoice in their Maker; let the people of Zion be
          glad in their King.
Let them praise his name with dancing and make music to
          him with tambourine and harp.
For the Lord takes delight in his people; he crowns the
          humble with salvation.
Let the saints rejoice in this honor and sing for joy on their
          beds.
May the praise of God be in their mouths and a double-edged
          sword in their hands,
To inflict vengeance on the nations and punishment on the
          peoples,
To bind their kings with fetters, their nobles with shackles of
          iron,
To carry out the sentence written against them. This is the
          glory of all his saints.
Praise the Lord.

Notice how the fetters are now being bound on the kings instead of thrown off? The nobles are in shackles of iron instead of breaking chains. Instead of plotting, there is praise. And in both passages, God is still God.

Chapter 2 – What is Theology?

For most of us, the answer to that question is, "The stuff that is stored in seminaries and cloisters, nunneries and monkeries (not a real word but coming soon to a dictionary near you), cathedrals, and basilicas around the world." But that is the furthest thing from the truth. Or, at least it should be. Theology should not be considered the ground that is hallowed beyond all common thought and kept by the gowned and robed men (and some women) telling the rest of us in the denominations of the world what we are to think about God, the Bible, and everything. If we were to follow only the Wisdom of Men – and their machines – without digging on our own, we would eventually be told that the "meaning of Life, the Universe and Everything" is 42.

In common definitions, we learn that anything that ends in "ology" is the "study" of something, and that is not quite right. It is close in that the "ology" comes from the Greek word, logos (λογοσ), which means "study," but more commonly it was used for; word, thought, speech, discourse, reasoning, judgment, and more. We get the word Theology by combining the "ology" with "theos," which is Greek for "god," so that we get a somewhat more personal and powerful definition when we apply all of that. What we have in Theology is what we Think (with Reason and Judgment) about God and matters relating to God.

I have long argued that all people are two things. They are all Theologians and they are all Philosophers. They may not be well trained in these disciplines, very bright about them, very well informed on them, very logical, or even reasonable, and most of them aren't really very good at them, but they are all Theologians and Philosophers. They may not even do it very often or with any intensity and tenacity at all. But it is true that they all think about God (even if only to deny Him), and they all stop to think about the meaning of life at some time or another. And if they get answers to some of their questions so that their curiosity is either satisfied or squelched, or if they are told that they cannot get the answers then sometimes they stop reasoning it out, and quit searching for the truth.

Some people are uninformed and not very prone to dig and research. These people tend to accept the first – or at least the early – answers they find, regardless of how simple, and regardless of how unreasonable. For example, if a high school or college student has reverence for his educators, and if they sell him on the idea that Evolution is truth – just because they sell so much and so hard – because of his trust in the notion that the teacher would only pass out truth – then he may buy into the idea without ever giving earnest consideration to any alternative again. This is especially true if the educational systems and entertainment industry have thoroughly indoctrinated the youth in the first place. If, from an Evangelical point of view, we know that people are most likely to make a life changing decision for Christ between the ages of 16 and 22, it is reasonable to assume that the enemy is just as likely to win him or her at that age.

At that age even the toughest youth is asking questions about his mortality and immortality and what it all means. If he is hanging out with a street gang, he is more likely to dismiss all of these considerations as fairy-tales that get

17

in the way of the business at hand, which may be sex, drugs, and turf. If he is at a liberal university, he is more likely to begin to worship at the temple of so called knowledge, and think that the wisdom of men can do anything. If he is sufficiently encouraged to do so, science may well become his god. Depending on his surroundings, it could be that his god is pleasure, achievement, money, power or anything – even another person.

Some people find themselves in church, and that can be a problem too. Not that going to church is a problem, quite the contrary – I have tried to make certain that my whole family has been in church almost every Sunday since we started a family by getting married. But what happens in many churches is that the people with lots of questions are being pastored by men and women who do not have a lot of answers, nor do they have the capacity or inclination to do the digging to help find the answers. The most common result is that the pastor will tell that questioning person that there are mysteries of God that can never be fully explained or understood, that they should just accept what they are told, and move on with their faith. Sometimes it is because the pastor doesn't want to look bad, or doesn't want to seem weak and un-authoritative, or just didn't know how to handle it, and so avoided it the best way he could. Sometimes it is because the pastor used to be one of those people with lots of questions and that was all that his pastor could tell him back in the day, so he is doing the same thing now. In many denominations this has become something of a hand-me-down paradigm. Either way, the enemy wins, and that is never good.

The Catholic Church has a standing tradition that is codified in most of its important documents that says that anyone can interpret Scripture so long as they do so in agreement with the "Magisterium." The "Magisterium" is the body of teachers in the Catholic organization, who speak with authority in matters of doctrine, and they decide what is right and wrong interpretation. The Catholic Encyclopedia Online[2] (http://www.newadvent.org/cathen/15006b.htm) says that the Magisterium has authority to validate such matters as infant baptism, papal infallibility, interpretation of Scriptures, prayers for the dead, Purgatory, and much more. This is further emphasized by the great Vatican II, which restates the validity and veracity of the Magisterium – as well as its function and power.

While those who know me will assert that I feel a strong sense of need for doctrinal correctness, they would also tell you that I abhor the idea of "Buying the Can;" especially when it comes to matters of grave and post-grave importance, such as Theology, Philosophy and Politics. This is especially true when matters of Theology are being decided, and sometimes dictated, by a bunch of old men who sit in a position to make decisions based solely on their having agreed with the previous bunch of old men who died and left them their jobs. In that I mean that there is little or no new thought (or even truly old thought) going into the process of declaring what is and is not right doctrine, only the process in which people are told the same old message. The "message" to which I here refer is not the Message of the Gospel, but the minor (and often errant) messages of what may seem of secondary and tertiary importance. Problem is that all too often those messages of seemingly lesser import alter and devalue the effect of the messages of greater import and even those of infinite import.

18

Example:

I was in a congregational meeting at a small Baptist church one night when they are discussing a possible merger with another congregation. They sent a series of questions to the pastor who could possibly be the future leader of the combined flocks. One of the questions was about who should receive the "Lord's Supper," to which the pastor had replied that he believed that "all Baptists should be welcome to the rite in their congregation." I made it a point of asking, "Why only Baptists?" and was met with a stern reply of, "That is a common belief among Baptists," at which point I voiced an objection on scriptural grounds, and one of the deacons told me, "Maybe you just need to become a Baptist."

While that may at first glance seem like a micro issue of simple deference, but there is nothing simple about it. This is a very real expression of doubt regarding another's salvation. Further, it is a thoroughly unnecessary affront. The Scriptures admonish the recipient of the rite to examine one's self, not that he is to be examined by the minister of the ritual. Can you imagine that Jesus or any of the Apostles expected that a pastor or assisting minister would be able to examine the heart of any, much less all who would come to the altar? This may be understandable if you knew that the person before you was living in sin, a drug dealer, or prostitute; but even that would not mean that they could never have come to the knowledge of Christ, and that precisely is the issue. If a person believes that Jesus has died as the only atonement for their sin, they qualify to receive the rite as much as any saint ever has. That singular belief is their only qualifier.

After the meeting, I asked the pastor to explain this position to me and his reply was that he didn't have to explain anything to me. But citing the words of 1 Peter 3:15, I claimed that Scripture required him to give an answer. It took a six page letter to the "deacons" to get the matter settled in that congregation, but that did not affect the general Southern Baptist Convention as a denomination. And it really didn't even settle it in that congregation, only that they would not exercise the exclusion while I was present and watching. I doubt that they continue now that I am gone.

How much difference can it make?

In the Sixteenth Century many of the debates of the Reformation were about what many would consider secondary or tertiary concerns, but they had profound impact on matters of primary concern. The most important thing to figure out is which matters are of "Primary Concern" and which are not. Once that is done we can figure out what impacts may result from our lesser concerns.

I believe that most Christians would agree that the Ultimate Primary Concern is: "How do we get to Heaven?" Once we figure that one out, we have to be able to work out whether any of the other issues we encounter have impact on that matter. And if so, how does it impact that matter of primary concern and how much?

If we teach that someone must be baptized (or re-baptized) to enter the Kingdom, the message is changed. One organization teaches that baptism is so essential that they also teach that the thief on the cross next to Jesus was baptized . . . by the rain. Now, nowhere in the Scripture does it say that it rained, but because they so firmly hold to the doctrine of "Essential Baptism," the thief must have been baptized in order to be saved, and so, it MUST have been raining when Jesus said, "you will be with me in Paradise."

Other groups teach that if you were baptized (as adult or infant) then you are saved, regardless of what you believe, how you live, or any other factor. This is most often shown at funerals and children's Sunday School classes. These groups also usually teach that baptism is not essential to enter the Kingdom, only Faith. But, somehow, if you are baptized the deal is sealed.

In the first case, baptism is essential and therefore it is a Work that must be performed in order to gain entry to Heaven. And isn't Faith without Works dead? In the second it is an easy doorway. Neither one is actually correct, however. Baptism is not essential, nor is it a doorway – but more about baptism in another chapter.

We were in one of the classes at Bible College when the discussion about Baptism and covenant led one of the students to say something like, "So, Baptism is related to circumcision, eh?"

To this the teacher replied, "If Baptism is related to circumcision then you open up a huge theological can of worms."

So my friend said, "Then Baptism is NOT related to circumcision."

And in reply, the teacher responded, "Then you are opening up a huge and completely different can of worms." But none of this stuff is actually simple. The Gospel is simple; Theology is work.

The point is that in none of these positions on the matter is completely thought out, neither is it thoroughly compared to Scripture to see, "What is the truth?" And that is what a Theologian should be doing. A good Theologian should be taking his or her own beliefs, and searching them out with Scripture and reason, to find what are the truths to be found in what he or she believes about God and in matters relating to God.

In the Scientific Method, the idea is to look at the evidence and formulate a hypothesis, and then try to prove your hypothesis FALSE! It is not to prove it TRUE. For the most part this is reasonable study and it requires just a few tools, foremost of which is willingness. The second tool is a good Bible – or two. I recommend the New International Version and the New American Standard Bible as the two best Bibles produced in the English/American language today. But more on that later.

How to Get It

Some of the passages in the Bible need to be "Culturally Contexted" – which means that they need to be seen in such a way as to consider the cultural setting into which they are written, but most of it does not. When the Bible says,

"If a man marries both a woman and her mother, it is wicked," (Lev 20:14) this passage does not need a context in a specific culture (except to notice that a man is apparently allowed to have more than one wife), just that these two women would have greater than common difficulty in the marriage arrangement. This is a statement that can be held "true" in just about all cultures and times. This is not so true when Paul writes to the Corinthians and says, "Does not the very nature of things teach you that if a man has long hair, it is a disgrace to him." (1 Cor 11:14) In this case there are some cultural realities that are not apparent in the text, like men with long hair and women with short hair usually serving (in that city and at that time) as temple prostitutes so that, the saying came about that men with long hair or women with short hair were doing "un-natural" things and had become "un-natural," so Paul could say, 'Does not nature tell you . . . get a haircut.' Paul is emphasizing that the things done by men with long hair and women with short hair are "un-natural" as the ways of prostitutes – usually men or women with either men or women. And there are even a few passages that may never be fully worked out before getting to Heaven and asking the author. One such passage is 1 Corinthians 7:36, wherein Paul comments about what a man does with his "virgin." The Greek text only says virgin, but translations add the words daughter, slave, or a virgin he is engaged to – but the text says only "virgin." Actually, none of the choices is perfect, but to me it seems that the choice of virgin slave fits the culture best and makes more complete sense; in the fuller context. Still the application and impact of this in today's culture is minimal at best. So, there is no need for a strong bone of contention.

I also want you to think of Theology as both a noun and a verb. Not only should everyone HAVE a theology, but each of us should DO theology. Anyone can have theology, and, as near as I can tell, everyone does. Many of us, as mentioned before, have a theology that has been handed to us in a "Can" by our denominations, parents, or culture. As far as this is concerned, we could just buy a book of theology by someone with a highfalutin degree and believe it – if we can read it. If you decide to do that, which I don't recommend, may I suggest "*A Theology of the New Testament*[3]" by George Eldon Ladd? While he and I don't agree on everything, he is, foundationally, a quality thinker who has reasons for what he believes – and I am confident that he is a Christian, not just a writer. Mr. Ladd does theology. But I suggest that you also DO theology.

Most denominations have a certain "canned" theology that ebbs and flows with the times and the culture in which they find themselves. If you are an American Baptist, you know that it is a sin to drink anything containing alcohol. But if you are a European Baptist, it is a sin to drink coffee. In Europe the water has long been a non-trustworthy entity and, as a result, beer and wine are a constant and a given. Children in Europe drink beer and wine at lunch and dinner, just like adults. But coffee has caffeine, which is a stimulant, and using stimulants is a sin – or so the European Baptists would have you believe.

An excellent example of how this worked out for someone in history is to be found in *The Puritan Dilemma: The Story of John Winthrop*[4] by Edmund S. Morgan. One of John Winthrop's burdens was that, as Governor of the Massachusetts Bay Colony, he was required to come up with a legal code for their

21

culture, and in doing so he felt convicted that "Sin" should be "Crime," and that to do this well, he must first understand what was and was not Sin. He was certain that if there were an action that was not a sin, but we called it a sin, the calling of it sin was a sin. To clarify, if we could find no scriptural evidence, mandate, or principle by which we call dancing a sin, then it would be a sin to call dancing sinful.

Who Should Do Theology

One of the most important things to learn is that there are a couple hundred snooty sounding words that you really don't have to learn. Don't get me wrong, if one wishes to become a Doctor of Theology (Th.D.), one must learn lots of these words and much more. But for each of us to get a better grasp of what God says and thinks and wants of us, we can keep the language down to a minimum. And if, somewhere along the way, you meet a theologian who uses words like Soteriology, Pneumatology, and Tetragrammaton; ask him what that big word means. If he looks down his nose at you in disdain, realize this one very important truth; he probably needs your prayers more than you need to know his big words. I say this in all sincerity because I have met a lot of people that know herds of fancy words and how to manipulate the Scriptures, but do not know God. Many of them have never met Him! That's right, there are unsaved Doctors of Theology out there, just as there are unsaved pastors and Sunday School teachers. I wish that were not so, but it is. But don't be surprised by this, there are thousands and more Professors of Business that have never run or owned a business.

If you are saved, and if you know and love God, you have a very real head start over a huge number of people that attend church or teach in seminaries. If you are tired of doing life your way, and are truly willing to be molded by Him in every aspect of your life, then you are miles ahead of most people with degrees and robes. And if you are willing to put in your own study time, and if you can be rid of your own excuses, then you have a very real chance of becoming who God really has in mind for you. But you must learn what He has in mind.

One of the things you can do is to enroll in a Bible College or Institute of some sort that is not of the same denomination you grew up with, for a year. In my case, I grew up in the Lutheran denomination and got saved in a Baptist tent meeting, but had little discipleship because of circumstances. Later I got into a Presbyterian Bible study class – that was rather liberal and later I attended an unaffiliated, conservative, Pentecostal school called International Bible College (IBC) in San Antonio, Texas for two years. I recommend at least a year, which is usually enough to get a good collection of fundamentals and learn to use some of the tools that are out there.

At IBC I got two semesters of the Life of Christ (five days a week), two semesters of the Pentateuch (Genesis through Deuteronomy – four days a week), a Survey of the Old Testament, Survey of the New Testament, Introduction to Prophecy, Introduction to Biblical Languages, Letters of John – along with a few other things. But what I got most was a stronger foundation in my faith and a familiarity with the tools. Using these tools I have spent much of my time building on that foundation.

The reason that I suggest an institute that is not of your own denomination is that you are already steeped in the denomination of your raising and know the way they think about most things, even if you do not know why they think that way. What is needed is an alternative view that is honest and open, and most importantly, non-coercive. You should not be forced to believe what I believe or what anyone else believes, but you should be given access to the tools that may help you find the elements of truth that have previously been unrevealed to you.

Note that I did not say "hidden" because that would imply that someone purposely concealed something from you, and usually that is not the case. We are not talking about some secret teachings, kept in check by the covert society, or some secret organization. We are talking about looking at matters from a different point of view. Also, we are talking about studying at schools that are decidedly Christian – not Mormon, Jehovah's Witness, Christian Scientists or Universalists – and I am also not even suggesting that you attend a Catholic school unless there is just nothing else available.

For additional input I recommend a variety of radio programs, not the least of which is "*Focus on the Family*," by Dr. James Dobson, as well as "*Truths that Transform*" with Dr. D. James Kennedy, and "*Thru the Bible Radio*" by the late Dr. J. Vernon McGee, whom all of us in theology love, though each of us disagrees with something or another he has said. Other great teachers are Dr. Chuck Swindoll of Dallas Theological Seminary and "*Insight for Living*," and Chuck Colson was one of the greatest mergers of Theological reality and Political thought, who left several books behind. There are hundreds of them, and I don't agree with any of them all of the time, but, for the most part, they hold sound and valid Christian views on most matters.

Reasonable Christianity

The first question in mind is, "What is Reasonable Christianity?" For some people, it is the idea that we as Christians should shut up and sit in the corner and don't bother anyone. For others, it is the idea that we may have certain beliefs that we show off on Sunday, but the rest of the week we should keep them to ourselves. In the political arena a reasonable Christian is one that has a "WWJD" sticker on his car but votes by the party line, whatever party that may be. In Hollywood a reasonable Christian is the kind of guy that believes in Jesus Christ, but would never tell anyone about Him, certainly wouldn't make anyone uncomfortable, and certainly wouldn't make a moral stand on anything done there. But for a true Christian, this is hardly reasonable.

Is it important to be "reasonable?" Well, that depends upon how you define reasonable. If it is defined by you as something resembling the first paragraph, then no, it is not important, because using that standard of "reasonable," there really isn't much that is important.

Scenario: Two men are standing in an office arguing about an ad campaign that may or may not include some women in skimpy clothing, making suggestive gestures, poses, and facial expressions. It "may or may not" because the two men are arguing about whether it should be so sexual at all. They go back and forth for a while, each expressing their vision for the ad, until finally, one of them says, "You really should be reasonable about this." What he is really saying is, "I want you to see and do this my way." Whenever you hear someone say, "You have to be reasonable" what they are really saying is, "do it my way." And when God says it, He means the exact same thing. But here's the difference; God always knows better. That is an important thing to remember, and it's important above pretty much everything. When God says it, there may also be a reward structure at play.

> Isaiah 1:18-20 (NIV) "Come now, let us reason together," says the Lord. "Though your sins are like scarlet, they shall be as white as snow; though they are red as crimson, they shall be like wool. If you are willing and obedient, you will eat the best from the land; but if you resist and rebel, you will be devoured by the sword." For the mouth of the Lord has spoken.

In this case God is speaking to Isaiah and in inviting Isaiah to "reason" He also includes rewards like the cleaning away of sins. For Isaiah's willingness and obedience he is offered the eats of the best of the land. This is a big deal because the best food of the land is had in the houses of the best and most influential people in the land. God is telling him that coming to see things God's way will result in the rewards of having the sins removed and then moving Isaiah into a new set of social circles. Remember that Isaiah spends much of his life in the company of kings. There is also a contrasting reward for resistance and rebellion. But, this is God's way throughout history; to offer the carrot and the stick about almost everything.

> Deuteronomy 30:19-20 (NIV) This day I call heaven and earth as witnesses against you that I have set before you life and death, blessings and curses. Now choose life, so that you and your children may live and that you may love the Lord your God, listen to his voice, and hold fast to him. For the Lord is your life, and he will give you many years in the land he swore to give to your fathers, Abraham, Isaac and Jacob.

There are countless passages that tell us that God offers rewards and punishment for choices and behaviours and some of them are immediate and physical, while others are eternal, ethereal, and spiritual. You can accept Salvation, on His terms, or go to Hell.

Sometimes we ask the wrong question. My family and friends were on a bus one Sonday, on our way to church. We were all dressed up in our Sunday Best and quietly singing praise songs in the back of the bus, as was our custom, and a man on the bus spoke to me. He said something, and I cannot recall his exact

24

words, but the bottom line was, "How could you believe in a God that would send someone to Hell for eternity?"

I looked at him for a moment and I told him, "You have asked the wrong question." He looked back at me, straight in the eyes, but a bit more intensely than before. So I said, "The right question is, 'Could you put your trust in a God that, could not have sin in His home, but wanted you there so badly that He would personally bleed and die to pay your price, and loved you and your freedom enough that He would still allow you to choose to go to Hell?' That is the question at hand." At that point the conversation had changed to where he knew that God did not send people to Hell, but that they were allowed to choose it. He now understood that the desire and goal of God is to have you at His house as an eternal guest, even as an adopted child, not to punish you for your life choices. This is God's ultimate goal, to such a degree that He lived a human life and died on the Cross as payment so that you and I could have access. If there is any decision to send us to Hell, that decision resides with us. So, I reasoned with the man and the seed was planted, and maybe some water sprinkled. I never saw the man before or since, but God has.

CS Lewis is said to have had his conversion experience while traveling – according to him – to the zoo with his brother. Further, according to Mr. Lewis his conversion was a matter of reason applied, yet to a certain degree unconsciously.

I know very well when but hardly how the final step was taken. I went with my brother to have a picnic at Whipsnade Zoo. We started in fog, but by the end of our journey the sun was shining. When we set out I did not believe that Jesus Christ is the Son of God and when we reached the zoo I did. I had not exactly spent the journey in thought. Nor in great emotion. It was more like when a man, after a long sleep, becomes aware that he is now awake.

All of the possibilities that he had considered in the past would swirl in his mind, just like yours and mine. We make decisions of lesser and greater import based not entirely on the immediate information we are provided on a matter, but on all of that information weighed on the scales and sifted through the sieve that is our life experience and knowledge. If that were not true then we would most certainly buy everything that every salesman in the world ever tried to sell us. But we take everything that we are told and we weight it and sift it and judge it and decide. We buy or we don't buy. We accept or we reject. Every decision has a lifetime's history and experience behind it, and that is what we work from, to, and with. Notice that Mr. Lewis said in his first line above "I know very well when but hardly how the final step was taken." It was a conclusion that began some time before and concluded at an identifiable time; at a moment in time, as it were.

This is the way God designed us from the very beginning. Each and every one of us is designed to make a decision. In the most important decision that we can make we are actually designed to accept the offer that God lays before us. He has put the Faith in us to accept it and He paid all the cost. It is the ultimate "win-win" deal. God created us to need Him, to please Him, to accept Him, and if we decide to reject Him, that is our decision to resist our design and His call. When God says that He wants to reason with you – and He really does want to reason with you every day – it means that He wants you to be reasonable, see things His way. He really does know best, and He really does love you.

Professor Richard Dawkins is a devout atheist and a virtual high priest of evolution, but in an interview on February 13th, 2012, Rev. Giles Fraser and Prof. Richard Dawkins, DPhil. discussed the findings of a recent survey conducted by the "Richard Dawkins Foundation for Reason and Science." In describing the conclusions of the study, Dawkins said, "The statistics purport to show that most people who identify themselves as Christian turn out, when questioned on what they actually think, to be 'overwhelmingly secular in their attitudes on issues ranging from gay rights to religion in public life.' Dawkins' conclusion, based on this survey information, is that these self-identified Christians are 'not really Christian at all'." But what right does an atheist like Dawkins have defining whether someone is or is not a Christian? After all; HE'S AN ATHEIST!!!

Further results of his survey show, regarding their reasons for alleging their own Christianity, "that fewer than three in ten (28%) say one of the reasons is that they believe in the teachings of Christianity. People are much more likely to consider themselves to be Christian because they were christened or baptised into the religion (72%) or because their parents were members of the religion (38%) than because of personal belief." If that were not bad enough, further details of the survey show that the "majority (60%) have not read any part of the Bible, independently and from choice, for at least a year." As greater evidence of his assertion, Dawkins survey revealed that "Over a third (37%) have never or almost never prayed outside a church service, with a further 6% saying they pray independently and from choice less than once a year." Continuing on the theme of prayer, "Only a quarter (26%) say they completely believe in the power of prayer, with one in five (21%) saying they either do not really believe in it or do not believe in it at all." The management of the "quotes" in that passage are from the study.

Now, I realize that this survey was among the "church" in England, people who checked the box to self-identify as Christians, but how much different are things really in America?

Come, let's be reasonable together.

Choosing Your Bible

Now, a couple of miles back I said, "I recommend the New International Version and the New American Standard Bible as the two best Bibles produced in the English/American language today." And I wanted to take a moment to qualify that statement, because I also don't want you to take what I have to say as another can for you to buy. I am not that important. The version that you choose is important though, because it is going to be a primary source for truth in your life in matters that matter. It will not be revealing the secret to well risen English Muffins, though they can be wonderful. It is a matter far more grave than that – in fact, it is matters even beyond the grave that will be addressed by your chosen version. Choose wisely!

The reasons that I prefer these two are their means of translation. One, The New International Version (NIV) is Dynamic, which means that they strive to accurately put into current language the ideas conveyed by the original texts, so that, while it is not as precise from a linguistic point of view, it is profoundly true to intent, from a life application point of view. The other, The New American Standard Bible (NASB) is said to be the most literal translation into current language, without trying to fit into current culture at all. It is just a very precise linguistic tool to see (as well as any translation can) exactly what the writers had to say. So, you can see that they are different types of translations, but their most important elements of translation are very much the same.

Their translators came from a variety of denominations on a voluntary basis – none of them was chosen by their denominations – and they worked with people of contrasting denominations. When a passage or chapter or book had been translated it was reviewed by others for soundness and rebuttal and reconsideration. When all feel confident that it is ready for publication, the "new" translation is sent out. This is where the real tests come about.

Once a translation is out there, the readers, pastors, professors, teachers and preachers, and ordinary people like you and I, send in a gazillion notes about what they think is handled improperly, or what is just plain WRONG with it, and all of that is reviewed. Then a newer revision is sent out and more notes are written and more reviewing is done, always with the idea that getting it right is far more important than making anyone happy. When a revision suggestion is made, the suggestion has to be evaluated as well and the text must be reviewed to see if the suggestion has merit, or if it just reflects a personal or denominational bias.

In the case of some of the more noted translations of the past hundred years, such as the Revised Standard Version, the New Revised Standard Version, the New American Bible and many others were translated by denominationally chosen people who had a predetermined theological agenda in mind when translating – as did the translators of the New World Translation, by the Jehovah's Witness organization. And if you start your translation looking for ways to further prove your personal or corporate theological views the whole work is tainted. It becomes your work, or the work of your organization, and is no longer a work of God. And finding the Word of God is the goal here, isn't it?

The Jehovah's Witnesses and the Mormons teach that if you can't use their text, the King James Version (KJV) is the only acceptable Bible. The reason is that some of the translational errors that exist in the KJV and language variances from common modern vernacular make the text more easily manipulated, because the more archaic language needs to be translated. In short, it is easier to use the KJV to twist the text and make the Word of God seem to say what they want. Some of the doctrines pushed by these cults are the divinity of Adam, polytheism, the spiritual finality of death for the unsaved, universal salvation, and much more. Again, choose wisely.

Picking out some Tools

Having selected a good translation, NIV or NASB, you may need to pick up a few tools along the way to help you get past some of the items in the text that are not so easy to understand because of 2000 – 3000 years of historical separation and lots of cultural difference. These tools can be had cheaply enough for the most part, and I recommend starting with a Halley's Bible Handbook, which can be had for anywhere between $5 and $30, depending on where and when you buy, and whether you feel a need for a new one, or if a twenty year old edition will do. I think my copy comes from the seventies.

Another thing that made a huge difference in my ability to do the digging that I wanted to do into the Scriptures is computer Bible software to put on your PC for a fraction of the equivalent paper library. Some can be had for free, while other packages cost as much as a couple thousand dollars – and may cost more for additional "add ins" that may be available. I got mine on eBay for less than half price, about ten years ago, and it has proven invaluable to me. But my first tools in Bible study were a couple of Bibles, NASB and NIV and a Walker's Comprehensive Bible Concordance, which goes for $5 to $20 – depending on when and where you find it. You may also want to pick up a few digging tools such as, Nestle Aland 26th Edition Greek New Testament with McReynolds English Interlinear, which puts the Greek and the English linear translation above and below one another, and then The New Analytical Greek Lexicon may help you if you can diagram sentences because it helps you break down the individual Greek words in their tense, voice and mood, and much more.

So, we need be saved and have an earnest desire to understand. We need a willingness to be changed and to become who God wants us to be and do what God wants us to do. We must be willing to do what is needed to learn what it is that God wants of us by willingly exploring what He has said in all generations – by finding teachers that are not like what we already have and hear. We must want to grow up and take some responsibility for the acquisition of knowledge and tools to acquire that knowledge.

> 2 Timothy 2:15 (KJV) Study to shew thyself approved unto God, a workman that needeth not to be ashamed, rightly dividing the word of truth.

We must find the Truth, learn it, sort through it, separate it and apply it in our lives. The Truth of God is like gold; remember that Jesus said that the Truth will set us free – but like gold, if we do not find it, learn to tell it from pyrite and to acquire it and apply it in our lives, it will do us no good. As gold cannot do you any good here if it is in a foreign land, in foreign hands – so the Truth cannot help you if you do not dig it up and make it your own. And it will not become your own if you accept it in the form of "leftovers" from people that may or may not have it themselves, or who serve only the parts they like, or who mix it with whatever else they may have. It will not be yours if you "Buy the Can."

By the way, Soteriology is the study of the theology of Salvation.

28

Pneumatology is the study of the works of God in the person of the Holy Spirit.

And the Tetragrammaton is the four letter Hebrew name of God, transcribed as YHWH, usually translated as Yahweh, and it is a name that has never actually been lost . . . this is what I call a semi-Christian myth, or a well meaning legend, which unfortunately resulted in the name being mistranslated by Jerome in the Vulgate, Latin Bible as Jehovah. Oops! Can I get a Witness?

Chapter 3 – Denominationalism – Good – Bad – Ugly?

Whenever one mentions denominationalism to a non-denominationalist the discussion is on. Some people are Congregationalists, and some are Presbyterian, while some are Papists and others are somewhere in between. But what does that mean?

In generalities these terms mean that they believe in various different forms of church government. For the Congregationalist, it means that he holds to the idea that the church should be governed by the congregation. Every decision is made by the group as a whole, from the call of the pastor and the mission statement to the drapes and carpet. Well, actually, they may select a committee for the drapes. But as a rule it is a true democratic organization. I don't mean that they are Democrats, though some may be, but I mean that the process is a genuine democracy – one person, one vote. The danger in this is that the crowd makes all decisions, and the crowd is only as informed as they want to be regarding matters of God. Sometimes the congregation is only a baby step away from street level understanding of the Word, and as such, they are prone to making bad, uninformed, ungodly decisions.

In the Presbyterian form of government, the elders (council – deacons – presbyters) make the decisions on a day to day basis, although, for the bigger matters, such as the purchase and sale of properties and planning a budget, there may be a contingency for a general or congregational election. Still, sometimes, the church's corporate officers are the council officers, and they have all legal authority to do as they will with any and all assets. This can be good or bad from a variety of angles, and for myriad reasons.

The Papists are, obviously, the Roman Catholics – though some would also include the Eastern or Russian Orthodox. In this case, the daily business is handled by local offices usually called Parishes. The greater matters of regional concern are handled by a diocese, or arch-diocese, which is presided over by Bishops. Above them are Cardinals and finally the Pope. In various places the names of the offices may be different to reflect the local language and culture, but the functions are the same. There is a hierarchy at play that is as rigid as any in military uniform. At the level of the Pope, there are traditions and methodologies that involve decision making processes that range in scope from group decisions by the "School of Cardinals" to speaking "ex-cathedra" – invoking the rule of "Papal Infallibility." This means that the Pope has the final voice in all matters Catholic, and his voice is irrefutable, even if it totally contradicts a previous pope.

In the Church of England – also called the Anglican Communion – the highest church officer is the Archbishop of Canterbury, but that office is overseen by the ruling Monarch of the nation – Queen or King at the time. So, in a real sense, the Monarch is the "Pope" of that organization.

30

So far, however, we have only looked briefly at structure, not the ups and downs of denominations themselves. The non-denominationalist would argue that denominations are sectarian and separating. They usually cite Jesus' prayer in the Garden for the unity of His people. Then they mention

> 1 Corinthians 1:11-13 (NASB) "For I have been informed concerning you, my brethren, by Chloe's people, that there are quarrels among you. Now I mean this, that each one of you is saying, 'I am of Paul,' and 'I of Apollos,' and 'I of Cephas,' and 'I of Christ.' Has Christ been divided? Paul was not crucified for you, was he? Or were you baptized in the name of Paul?"

They see denominations as being the same sort of divisions in the Church as Paul was discussing, but they fail to realize that they have separated themselves, by exercising their human right to separate in similar means as those denominationalists they have distained. Now, here is the deal. Just as I may choose to remain a Lutheran and you may choose to worship as a Baptist, the non-denominationalist, likewise, chooses to non-denominate.

As for what may be wrong with denominations, I submit that any time we strive to make a communized package, we weaken the truth. When we try to get a larger body to agree on the specifics of the faith, we tend to make allowances for personal or group preferences. For example, in some organizations the pastor is called a priest, and that priest may be referred to as "father" – which is directly contrary to the Word (Matthew 23:9). In another organization the pastoral persons may be male or female, but they may never have been divorced, basing that imposition on the passages of elders or bishops being the "husband of but one wife" – while Catholics deny that having a wife is allowed, still others believe that a wife and children are required. This is truly the down side of denominations. For the most part, the errors are usually of tertiary concern, or at least matters of secondary import. The primary matters are usually regarded in much the same way across the board. I have been a part of congregations that were Lutheran, Baptist, Methodist, Presbyterian, Catholic, Assembly of God, and more. I have been associated with Mennonites, Evangelical Free, Anglicans, Church of God, Church of God in Christ, and still more. In the essentials the differences are primarily that of what I would call "style."

John Wesley liked to quote Augustine that, "In essentials, unity; in non-essentials, liberty; in all things, charity."

All actual Christians believe that Jesus is God Incarnate, that His death was to pay for our sins, that the payment and forgiveness is available to any that will accept, free of charge, that it is the only acceptable payment for our sins and that every single one of us needs to be saved. Beyond that, it is mostly cultural differences. Some dance and some don't. Some have an orchestra, while others don't have any instruments in the congregation. There are those who clap and laugh and raise their hands, while others kneel and stand, kneel and stand a dozen times. Some even go to the front for "laying on of hands" or lay prostrate on the

31

floor or altar. They are all extremely different, but it doesn't mean that any of them is wrong. The only time they are truly wrong is when they add any other "must" to the Gospel, other than faith in Christ.

We sometimes get judgmental because not all people are like us. The ones that sit quietly in the pew and listen without a sound may not appreciate all the noise of a more ethnic Pentecostal congregation, with the occasional clapping, and singing, and laughing, the "Amen," and prayer out loud – and all without a script, program or liturgy. Conversely, many of the people that I went to Bible College with would go stir crazy in a Lutheran or Episcopal service – but can you blame them? After all, even the Episcopalians, Presbyterians, and Lutherans often call themselves "The Frozen Chosen."

The Up Side

Understanding that most denominationalism is simply a matter of style or cultural bias, and that the downfall of most denominations is normalization of things – and that stagnation is the biggest failing – there are still some serious benefits. The most important of the benefits is that of overseeing. Overseeing means that there is an element of accountability beyond the walls of the individual congregation. If people had been less ready to dump off denominations and more ready to overcome what may have been blandness or a need for change in the congregation of their raising, maybe there would not have been a Jonestown, the Branch Davidians, Heaven's Gate, and more. If people were better trained in the fundamentals of the faith and less eager to listen to the next new word, there would be no Mormons or Jehovah's Witnesses. There would be no Islam. There would be no Al-Qaeda. Weren't we warned that there would be teachers tickling ears?

The hard part is in realizing that the failing of what I call "anti-denominations" is that they often have little or no oversight beyond the walls of the single church, and sometimes they become their own micro-denominations. Sometimes that isn't such a bad thing. Sometimes it is. Sometimes a charismatic leader gets ahead, finds a following, and builds a large congregation that splits without enmity, where he is still the primary leader with what seems like branch offices. Now, I am not saying that this is, in all cases, a bad thing. In fact, it may even be a good thing more often than not. Hard to say! But it is best done when someone is watching.

Everyone should be watched over by people (not a person) who know better. When I say, "know better" I don't mean that they are smarter, or better informed than the smaller group. I mean "know better," like when your dad or my dad would say, "I thought that you would have known better." The idea is that the individual may have a novel insight, but the novel insight is hardly ever what should be the basis for a foundation on a new division or expansion of the Faith.

In practical terms, a foundational difference is what should cause a division other than a numeric split due to congregational growth. Even Martin Luther, after realizing God's intentions in "Justification," and after receiving and

32

sharing that understanding, he didn't just separate from the Church of Rome. He published his thesis, or it was published for him, as an invitation to talk about it.

Most denominations, and non-denominations, and even anti-denominations, split due to growth. Some congregations get huge before splitting, or just get huge and stay that way. From a practical point of view, the mega-churches are often a place to hide in the masses. For many people who prefer membership in a super church, the attraction to being in those pews is the ability to disappear. This is not true for all people. Some are there thinking that they will be able to be a part of using greater resources to do more work for the Lord. Some prefer the increased choices in Sunday School classes. Some churches offer three, or five or ten different adult Sunday School opportunities. According to a recent survey, another reason to attend a mega church is that a high percentage of church goers believe that the primary purpose of a church is to provide care and services to their families. This is another symptom of the "me-ism" that is so rampant in America today.

The Down Side

The preponderance of church and congregational studies indicates that the healthiest and most functional of congregations tend to be between one hundred and two hundred families, and the congregation splits between two hundred and four hundred families, into two congregations meeting in separate locations. Further, to keep from adding undue stress to the pastoral team of the "parent" congregation, the advantage of a denomination is that the "child" congregation can get direction and guidance from the denomination, instead of just from the prior pastor. Imagine the stress of having to parent two, three, or a dozen congregations, and what that could cost the congregation of the parenting minister as he is also supposed to be leading as a their pastor. It could easily become an administrative nightmare and that nightmare could easily destroy some ministry functions of a congregation and sometimes too much administration work can even destroy a good pastor.

The biggest down side of denominations is when they start to believe that they are the only true keepers of the Gospel. When they begin to think that everyone else is wrong and that they have the inside track; this is when they are usually on the way to getting lost. This is when they only allow their own to take the Lord's Supper or they have some unusual or additional requirements for baptism besides faith.

In case we all forget, here is the bottom line of the faith! I am a filthy sinner, unacceptable before God. Someone has to pay for my sin, and the price is Death. Jesus died to pay that price for me and nothing else, and I mean Absolutely Nothing Else is needed to buy my free access to Heaven. If you know and believe this, the rest is secondary, or tertiary or insignificant.

What is the Competition?

Some of the competition is listed above, but the primary competition is Satan. Whether you think of Satan as an individual evil entity overseeing a collection of evil beings of lesser importance, or if you view Satan as a collective of evil beings and evils as a whole is of less importance at this moment than simply that we perceive and understand that there is a source of evil and as we are reminded by Edmund Burke, who appears to have paraphrased John Wesley, "All that is needful for evil to triumph is that a good man do nothing." Burke said that what is needed is that "good men do nothing" but Wesley was certain that it was the singular man that surrenders victory to evil. This is true in our individual lives, but reinforced, as our good and evil are reinforced, in the lives of our culture or congregation, or any other collective to which we may be connected. But in the quote above evil is more of a generic term and sometimes the competition is quite specifically not a generic evil. It has a name, it comes with labels and we have allowed it to thrive, even in our midst. Here are but a few.

Evolution

The first two things to understand about evolution are these: 1. Evolution is the most misused and misunderstood term in common public discourse; and 2. Evolution as applied in schools as the means of the origins of life on this planet is a Religion, nothing else. But now, having said such allegedly ridiculous things, I have to support them somehow.

Regarding that the word evolution is misused and misunderstood, let's realize that there is a certain amount of "adaptation" – sometimes referred to as "micro-evolution" – that goes on in the world and within all species or else a mere change of climate or rain pattern could destroy so many living things. Darwin cited the black a white moths of his native England but upon further examination the black ones thrived where they could easily hide from predators in and amongst the coal dust, where as the white ones survived better where their colours assisted in their concealment. They were, however, two different moths that Darwin had hypothesized were the same species transforming from place to place. Darwin was wrong, though the thought of adaptation still exists, and reasonably so, but in this particular eventuality, the deity of evolution was wrong.

Adaptation explains why the African Elephant has larger ears than the Indian Elephant. Why? Because, the predators of the African Elephant come from farther away, and more quietly than do those attacking the Indian representative. There are about forty different variations of crows in the world, ranging in size from about that of a pigeon to the Common Raven, over three times that size, approximately twenty five inches in height. But all are crows with variations that allow them advantages in their given habitats. When my family went to the Grand Canyon, I awoke in the morning to the scuffle of two ravens, nearly two feet tall, fighting over something next to our campsite. They are the dominant carrion bird of the area. And with them pitching such a fit only twenty feet from me, I can tell you, they are a force to be noticed, even feared. But they are still only crows . . . BIG crows. And while an evolutionist may assert that millions of years ago they had a common ancestor, you do not have to choose to believe him. After all, it is only his religion and not at all the scientific fact that they would aver.

Bears come in only eight varieties today, but they really allow one to see diversity in specimens because of how well they hide in their natural habitats. Notice that the polar bear is almost all white. You and I can see a polar bear from miles away, due to our extreme colour sensitivity, but most animals don't see the shades of white that well, so by coming up on prey from the down-wind side and having feet so large and padded as to allow for some serious sneaking, they can snag some munchies most any day. Also, they are excellent fishers, and that ain't nothin' to sneeze at. Brown bears are, well, let's face it, pretty much brown. They fit into the scenery where they live, and if they are down-wind from you they will smell you and you won't smell them. Brown bears are also great fishers. In fact, the description of all bears, except pandas, is a camouflaged large stocky body, huge paws with non-retractable claws at the end of stocky legs, a long snout with huge teeth, shaggy fur, and a long winter nap. Pandas don't have to be well camouflaged because it takes very little finesse to sneak up on a stand of bamboo. But don't try to take that bamboo from him. Pandas are among the most dangerous animals to irritate, mostly because, like polar bears, they look so friendly and happy, but the claws and teeth are real. What I want you to understand most is that the bears are the way God made them, and all other things, for His purposes, many of which you and I cannot begin to explain. Some of it I get pretty well, but nowhere near all.

I cannot begin to explain cockroaches. I know that in the Bible it tells me that I have to destroy any crockery that is contaminated by roaches (Leviticus 11:33), so maybe their purpose for being is to help us always have newer crockery. Before anyone gets upset, that was levity. I understand ants and bees, most bugs and worms, cattle and chicken (yumm), but have a hard time with roaches.

As for Evolution being a religion, I want you to consider a definition of religion as being any belief or collection of beliefs that is supported more greatly by faith and assumption than empirical facts and evidence. Using this definition Evolution is far more a religion than Judaism or Christianity. For Judaism and Christianity the tenets of blatant faith are as follows: There is a Creative, Beneficent God. Everything else is either a record of evidence, testimony of eyewitnesses, or a logical result of that single, three-part assumption. There is a God – He is Creative – He is Beneficent. That is it.

The assumptions for Evolution are much larger than I can list here, but a short list may look like this.

1. All matter came into being incidentally – nothing exploded into everything.
2. Life came from non-life.
3. Mono-cellular creatures produced multi-cellular offspring.
4. Invertebrates produced vertebrates.

35

5. Water born creatures produced land born creatures.
6. Land creatures produced winged creatures, or water based creatures did it.
7. The list goes on, and on, and on.

When I was a kid in school they told us, as fact, that mankind had been around on the planet for about a million years, dinosaurs were a million years before that, and everything else had evolved into the current earth state in the prior two million years. Then scientists learned a bit more about the complexity of a simple cell and those numbers were changed. Man had still been around a million years, but now the rest of the world had been there for two hundred million. And then we learned some more about cellular complexity, amino acids, the intricacy of the galaxy and then they changed the numbers again. By the time I finished high school the word from the evolutionists was that the earth was at least ten billion years old, and man had been around for about a million still.

Back in the eighties, some mathematician whom I cannot recall said that the most elemental forms of life were so complicated that for life to occur randomly, given a billion instances of opportunity a day, would take over two hundred billion years to do so with any certainty. So, in a matter of thirty years the universe gained two hundred billion years, but there was also evidence on Earth that betrayed that thought entirely.

In Tarpley, Texas there is a place where a particularly unchanging mud exists. Once it is set and baked by the sun it cannot be remodeled at all. And in that mud there lays a dinosaur footprint, with a human footprint inside it. This is important to the dino-community because it shows a point in time where a human and a dinosaur occupied the same space on the same day. The importance is in the reality that it calls into doubt the "millions" of years, or billions that these evolutionists rattle off as fact. But just because someone can spout it doesn't make it true. And neither does it make it true to have it spouted from the front of a classroom.

A study of the silt deposits of the major rivers of the world helping to define the amount of dirt and rock being washed off the surface of the Earth, compared with the shifting of tectonic plates pushing land masses up creating more surface, results in an inequity so vast that if the speed of the tectonic shift were accelerated by a factor of 4 times, the surface of the Earth would still be completely washed into the seas in less than one million years. Enter the "Young Earth" theory.

Ever since the Scopes Monkey Trial of 1925 the American Civil Liberties Union (ACLU – also called the Anti Christian Libertines Union) has been struggling to make faith illegal in the market place of ideas, especially in politics and education. The ACLU picked up the bill for all legal services so that they could test their mettle against the Butler Act of Tennessee, which said that evolution could not be taught in a publicly funded school. And what has happened since has been an exact reversal of the Butler Act. Now, it is illegal, or supposed so, to teach Creation of any kind in a public classroom.

In the early 1960's the US Supreme Court ruled, in two landmark cases (Engel v. Vitale 1962 and Abington School District v. Schempp 1963), to end prayer in public schools, and the anti-God nature of public education was well under way. Since we began the process of trying to throw God out of the classroom, we have seen a steady decline of every form of decency in this country, worsening with each generation – including the decline in academic success.

In the fifties the big problems schools had to deal with were usually gum-chewing, cigarette smoking, truancy, and dress code violations, with an occasional pregnancy that was usually dealt with entirely by the families involved. The schools would never have considered that situation of a pregnant student their purview. Now, after fifty years, the biggest issues are kids killing kids at school, teachers having illicit affairs with students, homosexuality is taught as perfectly normal, sex is a how-to course, not a why-not course, and student pregnancy is so common that many school districts have pregnant and young mother schools where all of the students there are parents or parents-to-be. Drug use and drug deaths follow drunk driving and suicide as tragedies common to high school today. There have even been prostitution services run by administrators. It is so bad that having a "social disease" is considered a minor issue, and if a fourteen year old girl gets pregnant and the school officials get wind of it, they can spirit the girl away for an abortion without ever letting Mom and Dad know a thing. But that is what is to be expected when one thinks that mankind is the most important thing in the universe.

And that is not even the biggest problem with Evolution as a religion. One of the greater problems (but still not the greatest problem) of Evolution as a religion is that everyone involved gets to say that this person or that is more evolved than another, and is therefore more worthy of goods, services, protection, and more. It becomes a "caste" creating device based on any random element from education, to income, to political position, to genetics, and being born into the right social circles. Based on this aspect of the religion, some of us – politicians, academics and actors – would be more valuable than others. So, if some have to suffer for others to enjoy the lives to which they are entitled, that would be acceptable, after all aren't those who are the more valued among the Eloi? Isn't that what HG Wells envisioned as the important people, the Eloi, lived above the less worthy Morlocks?

Another problem that is rampant in the teachings of Evolution, and one that Darwin defined long ago, is the various "races" of mankind. Instead of seeing the Human Race as a single race of people, all with a single bloodline, all brown, of various shades, Darwin taught that the races of men were various levels of Evolution in man. He taught that the highest form of man was the Caucasoid (also called the Europoid), followed by the Mongoloid, the Negroid, and the Australoid. Darwin also postulated a future advancement in mankind to distinguish the future modern human far and away, more greatly separated from the animal world.

"At some future point, not distant as measured by
centuries, the civilised races of man will almost certainly
exterminate and replace the savage races throughout the world. At

37

the same time the anthropomorphous apes, as Professor
Schaaffhausen has remarked, will no doubt be exterminated. The
break will then be rendered wider, for it will intervene between
man in a more civilised state, as we may hope, than the Caucasian,
and some ape as low as a baboon, instead of as at present between
the negro or Australian and the gorilla."[5]

Some would aver that by "anthropomorphous apes" he means those he
considered less advanced of men, as mentioned in the final line.

Humanism

Humanism is the belief that mankind is the most important thing in the
world. It is a natural religious extension of the belief of evolution that assumes that
man has made the long climb up the evolutionary ladder and, as the highest form,
is deity over all others. In the Bible it rears its head for the first time at the Tower
of Babel.

> Genesis 11:3-4 (NIV) They said to each other, "Come, let's make bricks
> and bake them thoroughly." They used brick instead of stone, and tar for
> mortar. Then they said, "Come, let us build ourselves a city, with a tower
> that reaches to the heavens, so that we may make a name for ourselves
> and not be scattered over the face of the whole earth."

Dissecting that passage helps us to understand Humanism. First, they
conspired together as they "said to each other." Then, as is the Humanist way, they
decided to replace the natural supplies of God – stone – with the materials made
by their own hands – brick. After all, men know better than God how things
should be made. The primary purpose of the city was self worship. Cities in those
days were dedicated to their local deities, and at the heart of each of them was
some sort of altar, or temple, or sacrifice operation, if it is only a small shrine such
as stands in front of so many Catholic homes in South Texas. "Let us build
ourselves a city," is what drove their thoughts in creating this monument to
themselves. And what was to be the primary edifice of the place? They said it
would have a "tower that reaches to the heavens," which means that they would be
the intermediary agency between the heavens and the Earth. They could sit
between all mankind and deity, but also, if they reach the heavens, they become
deity. We are certain that their goal was not worship of God because of the final
sentence section; "so that we may make a name for ourselves and not be scattered
over the face of the whole earth." The ultimate goal of the work and the building
of the city and the tower was "to make a name for ourselves" and draw all the
people of the world to them. They sought to be gods. Further, weren't they
supposed to be operating under the orders of "filling the Earth?"
Little has changed from that day to this, but one thing stands out; now the
Humanists say that their religion is not a religion, and it has nothing to do with

38

God or gods at all, for there are none. According to Humanists there is no deity to obey, ignore or insult. It is just all a matter of some massive collection of freak accidents that resulted in the launch of life that evolved into the ultimately glorious Them.

The greatest problem with Evolution and Humanism is that, if we are all evolved then we are all somewhere along an evolutionary scale of development, somewhere between brutish beasts and perfected beings. If we are perfected beings then whatever we wish or do must be as perfected as we are, therefore cannot be sin. If we are not the perfected beings, but more like the brutish beasts, how could we possibly be held accountable for our actions by some arbitrary deity, such as God sitting in judgment over our sins?

But, since the Human Being has become the culmination of all that is worthy, and is now the god of this world, it is incumbent upon this god to tend to the needs and show better stewardship of the home of his creation, the Earth and all that he now surveys. This is the more human side of the culture and religion of Environmentalism, but there is another.

Environmentalism

The idea of wanting to care for the Earth and all it contains as a resource that must be better managed goes back several thousand years, even to the ways of respecting life and property as defined in the Bible. But today's Environmentalism is a much more complicated, and often a far more convoluted creature. I call it a creature because it is not actually a system but a self-developed organism of thoughts and behaviours all around the world by everyone from Cub Scout troops that adopt a highway to multibillion dollar enterprises making hay on the good will of people being duped into "buying the can" from the peddlers of pop culture and political pandering.

In its simplest forms, being an environmentalist is not a bad thing. It encourages good stewardship of the gifts that God has provided. It teaches us to properly use things, to clean up after ourselves, and to use what we need, not all we can. In this form of environmentalism, or what Christians call stewardship, we distribute trash cans, and even recycling bins, all over cities and parks, so that people can dispose of their refuse while out and about, without trashing up the place. We also drive less, try to use more efficient vehicles, and keep them in good working order. We may use biodegradable diapers and paper towels and grow some of our own foods and we may even can them in glass.

But sometimes that message is taken to such extremes that belief in the "system" becomes impossible. Then it morphs into a political tool that becomes oppressive and unmanageable by those under its thumb. It becomes the Environmental Protection Agency (EPA) and invades every aspect of life and business, and it does so with such super human foolishness that it could never have been imagined when it was created. If it had been imagined, I doubt whether anyone would ever have signed off on it.

In the best of times the San Joaquin Valley of California provides about twelve percent of the produce of the United States and jobs to countless thousands of people in the agriculture business and the support industries. In 2009 there was found to be a delta smelt population near the pumps that provided the irrigation to the valley, so the pumps were stopped. In the months that followed the legal melee and economic nightmares was astounding. Crops began dying from lack of water and food that would have ended up on millions of tables simply did not come into being. Further, about 50,000 people would be out of work within a few months because the harvest was extremely light and the people usually needed to maintain the fields as the crop matures could not be paid because there was no harvest coming. Restaurants and gas stations saw their business levels decrease drastically, but we had to make certain that the estimated 300 to 350 of these three inch long fish were protected, regardless of the damage to human lives, families, and enterprises. Realistically, a smelt cook-off could resolve the entire matter and the food production could resume and employment in the area could climb and costs of groceries could come down, but we have to protect these fish. Or do we?

We know that over 150,000 different species and sub-species have become extinct, with only a relative hand-full of them disappearing by human agency. But whether they disappear because we hunt them down, like dodo birds, or because they run out of space to live, like these smelt, we have to consider their contribution to the whole. After all, part of the environmentalist movement is that idea that everything is needful for the planet to work properly. But, if that were actually true then everything would have been thrown completely out of whack with the demise of the first species to go to "dodo-land." But the world didn't spiral into chaos when dodos died, so we have to assume that there is some flexibility in that concept. The flexibility in the concept can be understood in these words: "the world adjusts." Even though Mauritius, the home of the dodo, was overrun by humans bringing monkeys and rats starting in about 1505 and the last dodo seems to have died in 1681, along with another twenty plus species of birds that lived only there, the ecosystem of the area continued to thrive without them for another three hundred years before the place got converted into giant tea farms and sugar plantations. The point is that with at least thirty species removed from the operational ecosystem of the island, things changed drastically, and the work of continuing to live kept on chugging along. Creatures bred and died, animals continued to eat one another, they pooped and their remains rotted and the ground was nourished and life continued. Even without these creatures, regardless of how beautiful or ugly they may have been. In the words of Dr. Ian Malcolm (played by Jeff Goldblum) in the movie Jurassic Park[6], "I'm, I'm simply saying that life, uh... finds a way."

In an episode of the Showtime program, *Penn and Teller: Bullshit*[7] they revealed an interesting factoid. Now, I don't usually recommend these guys for their accuracy, but, I looked around and found this tidbit to be interestingly true. If you took all of the landfills in the world and put them in a single place, the area of that landfill would be about thirty-five miles square, which 1225 square miles, or in Texican terms is 784,000 acres, or about one third of the size of Yellowstone National Park, which is 2,219,791 acres. So, if that is the case, and it is, then we have less trash in the world than could cover some ranches in Texas. In fact, it could all fit on the King Ranch. Don't get me wrong, the King Ranch is an enormous enterprise, but in comparison to the surface of the Earth, it is a speck. Penn and Teller also showed now much of the recycling operations are little more than a huge money grab from the Government, meaning you and me. Please don't misunderstand, some of the efforts are good, working, productive and even profitable; but much of Environmentalism is none of those.

Another thought to keep in mind is that in the 1960's we had the "Anti-War Protestors," college students that were calling for the end of the Viet-Nam war. But underlying their movement was a huge wave of Socialism that led to a lot of "Commune" living, or limited and encapsulated Communism. This was usually quite separate from any of the Jesus Freaks for ideological reasons. The idea was to keep to themselves and avoid all involvement with the Capitalist culture that was America, and to protest the actions of the nation in other parts of the world. There were underpinnings of Marxism and the desire to move from small communes to the greater commune. When the war ended in the seventies their protest movement morphed into different forms, and they moved from "keeping to themselves" to cultural infiltration.

Many of these students saw that their best way to effect change was to enter the world of Academia, so they became the replacements for the Marxist professors they idolized. Others began protesting a new found evil that was rearing its head in the sixties with the publishing of a book called *Silent Spring*[8], by Rachel Carson. It began making the rounds in the early sixties and although it was one of the most poorly reasoned, worst researched, and least scientific documents since the *Origin of the Species*[9]. It was however, well received among the academic elites and Socialist dinner parties. It was compelling. It got President Kennedy to have his Science Advisory Committee to investigate the claims of the book. But the Committee gets its investigative material from the Marxist elites and academics that love the philosophy of control over anything, so they validate the book and the regulations begin. And the "Environmental Movement" is born. The hippies and protestors of yesterday and their children, become the political machine of today, and through a combination of Academia driven Marxism, Social Justice, and Liberation Theology, followed by a touch of Fascism – led by the liberal media – the Democrat Party, and even a little bit of honest to goodness concern for the environment; but not too much.

Government

Another problem with Environmentalism is that environmentalist force their agenda on more people through the Government than anyone should be able to. If you have a pre-1970's automobile it really needs the lead in the fuel to perform correctly, but you can't buy leaded gas at the neighborhood store, so you have to use an additive that *almost* does the trick, while making your engine run dirtier. In most cities you have to pay a sewage fee with your water bill, and you have to use the sewage system to rid your home of waste, even though a properly

41

managed septic tank and gardening is a better answer for the environment and your wallet. But that would take a finger of government out of your lives, and government doesn't want that, ever.

Environmentalism becomes Governmentalism when government begins to create policies, based on "Environmental Science" that is neither environmental nor scientific, in order to control more of the lives and daily functions of the populace that government is supposed to serve. But the government has forgotten the part about being the public servant and is growing out of control to where it is becoming the public master. When I was young there were people, and still are some, who were worried that the world would be taken over and run by the corporate conglomerates. But now, the ones that are still concerned about that are making sure that it never happens by turning government into the monster they always feared corporations may become. It is like watching some sort of twisted *Terminator*[10] movie and everyone involved is trying to build the machine world that will take control of, and eventually destroy the human world.

The environmentalist is worried that I am going to rape the earth with my desire to build a new car, while the government is worried that if I build a new car then I will become more autonomous and want to run my own life, and teach people to do the same by providing opportunities and jobs that would then allow people to spend their own money on their own desires and needs, instead of being on the public dole and relying upon the government to provide their needs and keep them in check. But in the environmentalist's desire to protect the planet from me, he has abdicated his own life and will to the government that he believes will provide his global protection. He has been convinced that by the empowerment of the EPA, and other governmental agencies that he sees as protective, that the world is going to be a better, cleaner place, healthier for all. But, he doesn't see the agenda behind the agenda. The EPA and others are like the Ministry of Truth from George Orwell's *1984*[11], in that their name belies their function. The purpose of the EPA is to gain governmental control under the auspices of the protection of the environment, like the Ministry of Truth's primary purpose was the dissemination of the lies of Big Brother and call it news and public information and the like. They are like the most liberal of the press who never present a counter concept clearly, but worship continually at what is currently the Democrat machine and their high priest and prophet, BH Obama. "Come, let us build a city for ourselves."

Islam

Islam is right after government and right before a couple of other religions because it is a political ideology that is presented as a religion. About fourteen hundred years ago a guy called Mohammed looked out in his world and saw Christianity and Judaism as the dominant religions and found them lacking in discipline and political authority, as well as organization and benefit to the most important person he knew; himself. Realizing that Christianity was the reasonable, rational, and supernatural offspring religion of Judaism, he determined that what was needed was another (alleged) offspring from Christianity, so he devised a

42

means by which he would simply decry the predecessors as deficient and defective, having had their Scriptures scrambled centuries before, and with him as the True Prophet of God having been sent to correct the errors. He taught that the Christians had misinterpreted the Scriptures, as had the Jews, and that they had both conveyed the holy texts erroneously, and often with malice of forethought for an intended result, declaring all of the theology of the West – anything West of him – as a fraud. I will agree with Mo that there has been some misinterpretation of Scriptures, but fervently disagree that the original language texts are corrupt in any way. But more on that later.

As he develops this "religion" he writes the Qur'an, his own testament and makes God over in his own image, and to make certain that no one confuses his god with the God, he makes everyone who believes him call their god, "Allah," meaning "the god." It is a name that is known in his cultural and linguistic circles for its meaning and it is adopted pretty quickly. And it has been on the grow for the time since. In fact, it is one of the fastest growing religions in the world.

We must fully understand the elemental differences between Islam and Christianity. The ultimate goal of Christianity is to tell the world about God and what He has done for every one of us through Jesus' life and death on the cross and resurrection. The ultimate goal of Islam is to, literally, rule the world for Allah. Its central theme is the doctrine of Global Hegemony, and it means that in the end there will be a world of three kinds of people; First, the Islam or Muslim, who are the believers and followers of Allah and Mohammed through the Qur'an, Second, is the non-believing servant class who will be forced into submission and servitude to tend the needs of the believers, Third, the infidels, who are to be killed and who come in only two classes. As an infidel you can be either dead, or waiting to be dead.

Another thing to realize about Islam is that, as a Muslim, you can only commit a sin against a person, and only a Muslim is a person, so you cannot commit a sin against a non-Muslim. To lie to an infidel is not a sin, but rather a duty to a Muslim. In fact, anything that a Muslim can do to inconvenience or destroy a competing form of government must be done, unless it is a place where the Muslim is outnumbered or they cannot get away with it. Seriously, there are passages in the Qur'an saying such things. If you have a Muslim neighbor who tells you that they are part of a religion of peace remember that it is not a sin to lie to you, unless you are a Muslim.

A note about fairness is needed here because "fairness" is all the rage now. It is also a bunch of crap, but it is all the rage. When someone says that we have to be fair, and 'can't we all just get along' what they mean is that you have to accommodate them somehow. But that's not fair either. In America we have to make all kinds of accommodations to keep Muslims happy and not violate our own sensibilities about fairness, but they don't. In some airports there have to be foot washing fonts for Muslim taxi drivers, but in Muslim countries it is not uncommon to find it is illegal to be a Christian, and proselytizing is punishable by death. In America we have businesses that have had to make accommodations of time and space for five prayer cycles a day, but in Turkmenistan you can only have a church if you get a permit, but getting a permit is impossible due to the convolution of the process and the time limits and delays, and police raid home churches and arrest members for not having the proper permits. In Pakistan blasphemy laws are so restrictive that if for some reason you deny the Prophet Mohammed, you should expect to be arrested and imprisoned, even punished by death. If you treat the Qur'an with anything other than holy reverence or preach from it to show the errors of it, you can be imprisoned for life. And don't ask what happens if you write in it. In Malaysia the law reads "Parliament may, by law, make provisions for regulating Islamic religious affairs." But according to the rest of the law any and all religious affairs are Islamic by definition because, "Islam is the religion of the Federation," according to Article 3 of their Constitution.

Please, if you don't take any other eye-openers away from this discussion, please be aware that Islam is not a religion of peace, but a movement of death and destruction. To deny this is to attempt to hide more than millennium of history, including the 9/11 attacks. It is a religion-wrapped political philosophy that is about control. The Ottoman Empire held every inch of land from modern Turkey, South and across Northern Africa, and across the Strait of Gibraltar into Spain. They got that control and kept it from about 1300 AD to the end of World War Two by killing people that got in their way and disbelieved their god. There has never been any tolerance in that religion and there never will be.

Some people point to the Spanish Inquisition and say, "See, the Christians are just as bad." But, they fail to realize that the Spanish Inquisition lasted a total of three hundred sixty years, but was only fully operational for about a third of that, and it was an agonizing blight on the world for about half of that time. And a huge part of why it could live so long, and thrive as it did was because of the centralized religious government headquartered in Rome, fighting against the ongoing threat of the Ottoman Empire and Islam that surrounded them on three sides. Also, don't be so foolish as to compare less than a century of Inquisition to more than a millennium of jihad

Mormonism

Now it may seem strange to put Mormonism right next to Islam, but I want to begin by checking your knowledge. How many of you know that the first religious terror attack on American soil took place on September 11th? How many know that the September 11th in question was 1857, called the "Mountain Meadows Massacre" wherein about one hundred twenty men, women and older children were killed for their wealth in both property and cattle, and for passing through the Utah Territory? The Utah Territorial Militia got some of the nearby Paiute tribe to join in and laid the blame on the natives. But it was the local Mormon fellowship that had committed the acts. Depending upon who you ask, the militiamen may have been acting of their own volition, but most reports of the time say they did very little without the instigation of Brigham Young.

An essential distinction of Mormonism that is most difficult to align with Christianity is not their has-been practice of plural marriage, but the rest of the collective doctrine of the organization. For starters, the Mormon faith teaches that

44

Adam, the human father of all mankind, is also the deity of this planet, known as Elohim. With his first celestial wife, Eve, he populated the Earth, and with another celestial wife, Mary, he begat Jesus by sexual intercourse. Jesus was born so that he could represent his father's interests and contrast those interests of his brother, Lucifer, also called by many, Satan. Further, the Mormon church teaches that they are the only true church of God on Earth.

> Doctrine and Covenants Section 1:29-30 And after having received the record of the Nephites, yea, even my servant Joseph Smith, Jun., might have power to translate through the mercy of God, by the power of God, the Book of Mormon. And also those to whom these commandments were given, might have power to lay the foundation of this church, and to bring it forth out of obscurity and out of darkness, the only true and living church upon the face of the whole earth, with which I, the Lord, am well pleased, speaking unto the church collectively and not individually.

That passage is from the Book of Doctrine and Covenants, which is the final authority to practitioners of Mormon theology. The Mormons teach that if you can't use a Bible of their publication then the King James is the only one suitable, and that the Book of Mormon is the final testament of the Bible, and the Book of Doctrine and Covenants is the explanation of it all. But, it is not like the Book of Concord to the Lutherans – which is an insightful interpretive tool. The D&C is said to be inspired, like Scripture, to be the be-all, end-all of everything. When in doubt, check with the D&C. But, did you notice that part where it said "the only true and living church upon the face of the whole earth?" That is not some sideline teaching like the Baptist thinking that they are the only ones to get it all right. No, the Baptists still allow that the rest of us are part of the faith. The official Mormon position is that if you are not Mormon, you're not Christian. Mormons don't claim to be Catholic or Protestant, but the only version.

One of the huge differences between Mormonism and Christianity is that Mormons believe that if you are a good Mormon, and have enough wives and kids, and if everyone is good enough according to the church, a man and his wives can become gods – as well as the Adam and Eve – of their own planet and their children can be the devil and messiah of their worlds. Now, I don't know the magic number of how many wives and kids it takes, but wouldn't that be a target to shoot for?

Another of the odd doctrines of Mormons is that everyone that is not either a murderer or an ex-Mormon gets into some level of Heaven. In this case having a relationship with God or Jesus is of lesser importance because the avoidance of the punishment has already been arranged. Adam, the "father god" has arranged it to be so. Of course this is not in agreement with such passages of Scripture that harp on that whole One and Only God idea.

Three passages that draw my attention to that idea are as follows:

Isaiah 41:4 (NIV) Who has done this and carried it through, calling forth the generations from the beginning? I, the Lord—with the first of them and with the last—I am he."

Isaiah 44:6 (NIV) "This is what the Lord says— Israel's King and Redeemer, the Lord Almighty: I am the first and I am the last; apart from me there is no God.

Isaiah 48:12 (NIV) "Listen to me, O Jacob, Israel, whom I have called: I am he; I am the first and I am the last.

Also, did you notice that part about the first and the last? Doesn't that remind you of those Alpha and Omega passages of the Messiah, Jesus speaking in the book of Revelation?

Revelation 1:8 (NIV) "I am the Alpha and the Omega," says the Lord God, "who is, and who was, and who is to come, the Almighty."

Revelation 21:6 (NIV) He said to me: "It is done. I am the Alpha and the Omega, the Beginning and the End. To him who is thirsty I will give to drink without cost from the spring of the water of life.

Revelation 22:13 (NIV) I am the Alpha and the Omega, the First and the Last, the Beginning and the End.

If God claims to be the first and the last, the beginning and the end, and Jesus claims the same thing, either they actually are the same, or someone is a liar. This is an important bone of contention to the Mormons, but even more so to the next cult that believes that Jesus is actually the Archangel Michael.

Jehovah's Witnesses

They go door to door and put up with more verbal abuse and dismissiveness than a Conservative Christian in Hollywood, preaching at a brothel, or worse, at the Academy Awards. Too bad they don't actually have the truth on their side. The first non-truth is that Jesus is Michael. I really don't get that one. But first, a reference.
In the first passage we see Jude giving validation to an old saying about the disposal of the body of Moses,

Jude 9 (NIV) But even the archangel Michael, when he was disputing with the devil about the body of Moses, did not dare to bring a slanderous accusation against him, but said, "The Lord rebuke you!"

46

From this passage a JW may say that only Christ has the power to dispute the devil, therefore, this must be Jesus being called by the name Michael because that is who He is. But that is not who He is. Remember this: (James 4:7 NIV) "Submit yourselves, then, to God. Resist the devil, and he will flee from you." So the idea that only Jesus can dispute the devil falls along the wayside. It doesn't require much because even someone as useless as I can do it.

In the second passage we see where they get their misunderstanding of this identification, because of the bad use of language and the mishandling of the Greek text they see Michael and his angels fighting against the dragon and eventually tossing the dragon out of Heaven. The dragon is identified as the ancient serpent, the devil, Satan, who leads the whole world astray. The next verse says that the salvation and power of the kingdom of God has come with the authority of Christ and they confuse the authority of Christ with the power of Michael and conflate the two into one. The language of the text really does not allow for the confusion, except in bad translation, and misinterpretation.

> Revelation 12:7-10 (NIV) And there was war in heaven. Michael and his angels fought against the dragon, and the dragon and his angels fought back. But he was not strong enough, and they lost their place in heaven. The great dragon was hurled down—that ancient serpent called the devil, or Satan, who leads the whole world astray. He was hurled to the earth, and his angels with him. Then I heard a loud voice in heaven say:

> "Now have come the salvation and the power
>   and the kingdom of our God,
> and the authority of his Christ.
>   For the accuser of our brothers,
> who accuses them before our God day and night,
>   has been hurled down.

For starters, the power of Michael is not directly mentioned, only that he and his angels fought against the dragon and his angels, and were victorious. Remember that the word "angels" means "messengers." At times these messengers have also been warriors, but when the word angel is applied in Scripture, the holiness of that creature is not to be considered as a given, except using the original definition of the word "holy;" which is "set apart." We assume, erroneously I should add, that it automatically means "set apart for God." Sometimes holy means "set apart FROM God." Linguistically, it just means "set apart."

The Witnesses also believe that your Salvation has to be earned and kept. Because it is dependent upon you to get it and keep it, Salvation becomes a prize that you have earned, to the detriment of your relationship with the Lord. Conversely, if you fail to keep on the straight and narrow, you could lose your Salvation and be damned for checking out that waitress at Jim's.

Another odd thing about the Jehovah's Witnesses is the idea that there will be super-elevated positions of reward for One Hundred Forty Four Thousand

47

people that are the best evangelists in the history of the Church. The really interesting thing about this is that they claim to get the idea from the book of Revelation but nearly none of them could begin to qualify. You see, the entire group is made up of Virgin Jewish Males. Yes, virgins. Yes, Jews. Yes, males. There are twelve thousand from each of the twelve tribes of Israel and they are men who "have not defiled themselves with women." It has nothing to do with being evangelists or earning a space in the best neighborhood of Heaven, but it is a point that there will be these evangelists, from that people, Israel, in that vast number and their goal will be the change of heart and mind of the world. Just another clue; they will fail. Not for lack of trying, but because there will always be someone that will not take the offer.

Chapter 4 – Fidelity, Love, Matrimony and Monogamy

This is my brief treatise on marriage in which I especially intend to discuss what it is, should be, is not, and should not be. Before we get started in this arena, however, I wish to point out that every reader of this book, and indeed, this passage, will read this material from their current cultural, political, and historical point of view. And we all need to recognize that truth.

The reality that this addresses is that of 'what you see is what you expect should be.' And while this may, at first, sound fair and simple; it becomes complicated by the fact that our individual thoughts on important items are usually assembled, in great part, by the thoughts, statements, and displays of our family and culture. In the typical and modern American picture the influences are (in descending order) TV, movies, videos, internet, church, politics, school, home, newspapers, etc. This is not a small or even limited package of input providers. One hundred fifty years ago, that list may have been pretty much just home, church and school, in that order, but now, the plain volume of influences and the scope of influence they wield is too vast to measure. Add to that the fact that along with those influences, there are music, billboards, commercials, and subliminal messaging as well as subtext, and it becomes a plethora of philosophical poisoning. However, there are some simple and generalized norms that can be labeled and stated. And that – the simple norms – is where we begin. In the following chapters we will briefly examine Fidelity, Love, Matrimony and Monogamy; the commonly perceived elements of Marriage in the Judeo-Christian, Euro-American cultural understanding.

If we look at the typical American understanding of marriage the picture is a man and a woman and a vague number of kids. Optimally, or so it is thought, this couple meets in High School or College; they date for between six months and two years and they tie the knot, make babies, raise the kids, and grow old together 'til one of them dies, followed shortly thereafter by the other. However, that is the optimal, not the usual, common, or typical.

Fidelity

Many people in America have come to discount and dismiss marriage in favor of a "loving and committed relationship." This is even a phrase used to describe a homosexual relationship when they want it recognized as marriage, but no one is honestly buying into the idea. What this phrase really means, and the way it should be translated is: "lots of loving (to be read as sex) and commitment (remembering to come home to the same place tomorrow) where two people agree to stay together . . . 'til some later time." The problem with that kind of commitment is that there really is no genuine commitment.

So, the guy in the relationship may say, "Of course I'm committed to my girlfriend." But he can't get to the point of commitment where he can refer to her as his "wife." Why? Because, regardless of all he says about there being no difference, he is absolutely certain that there is a difference. He can claim that he is just as bound to his girlfriend as another is to his wife, but deep in his heart and soul, he knows that this is not true. He wants you and me, and especially the "girl" to think that it is all the same, and that is why he doesn't have a wife. He knows that if she is a wife, she has a different relationship with him, a different position in the culture, and a different personal, positional, and legal status. As a wife she has a claim. If she is his wife, she is entitled to certain evidences of his care and concern and protection. If she is the girlfriend she has a right to walk. And, the same is true for him . . . as long as she is not his wife. And that is not really much of a commitment, by either one of them; is it? Or, to rephrase; they remain bound to one another, as long as they both may leave!

The next thought on that is, "Well, as long as they are both only that committed, then their arrangement should be just fine. After all, aren't they both getting what they want?" Unfortunately, the answer to that question is, "No," because in reality, neither one of them is actually getting what they want. No, at least not as much as they hope for. Yeah, there is sex; but is the sex alone even all that it could be? And, yes, there is companionship; but isn't that self-effacing/other-serving form of companionship really what they want? If there is the ongoing expectation that the other may leave, could depart, or is going to leave, is there ever real and true sharing and trust? And without truly deep and intimate sharing and trust, even the sex finds limitations, because truly powerful and dynamic intimacy can only be had with profound trust and confidence in one's partner. And that only comes when each partner expects that the other is going to be there, more than just today or tomorrow – or this year – and that the partner will not reject them for their desires. This is strong trust. This is true fidelity.

What we have to understand is the definition of Fidelity. Fidelity comes from the Latin word, *fides*, which means "faithful" – or trustworthy; worthy of reliance from another. That means that your partners in life, love, business, and whatever else can trust and rely on you. It means that you can rely on each other. And, isn't that worth a bit more? Semper Fi – or Semper Fideles – is the motto of the Marine Corps, and if you ask a Marine, its importance is staggering and its bond is life changing. Once a Marine, always a Marine!

Another major problem with Fidelity in America is the assumption that everyone is going to cheat in their relationships. It is like most public funded "abstinence" programs that are actually like the Sex-Ed class on the movie *Mean Girls*[12]. The teacher says, "Don't have sex or you will get pregnant and die. Okay, everybody, come up here and get some rubbers." See, that's a huge problem. Everyone is being trained to expect failure – or should I say that we are being trained to fail? After President Clinton had an affair with an intern the most liberal press outlets began dismissing it all by saying that "everyone cheats" some time or another. To prove their point, several of the liberal publications even did anonymous surveys of their readers in the following few months and years, to see what percentage of their readership actually had cheated, either in marriage or a "loving committed relationship." And, across the board, the answer was right around 30% - some slightly higher, some slightly lower. So, apparently, not everyone cheats; in fact, most don't. Now, remember that it was liberal publications doing the studies – not conservative ones. These publications were taking surveys from people who have a sociological predisposition to deny any idea of an absolute right and wrong, and still, even among these people it is less than a third. I cannot help but wonder what the percentages would have been if they had also managed to survey some practicing Baptists, Catholics and Pentecostals. It's just a thought.

Now, please realize that this indoctrination to expect failure in fidelity is like any other training program in that not all participants are aware for their involvement, and not all participants are successful in their progress through the training program. Realize that there were people trained in 1930-40's Germany to be excellent little Nazis, but some did not buy into the whole package. Some, like Dietrich Bonheoffer, reasoned their minds to keep free from the poison that the Nazis were injecting into the German culture. And others, while not so successful at breaking thoroughly free and rebelling against the evil tide, may not have succumb fully to the persuasion of the propaganda. The same is true here. Some people will learn the truth and some will rebel against the evil – and some – just don't buy it all and never fall victim to the traps. At the same time, they don't manage to spring free from all the snares either, just managing to avoid the most heinous ones. Another thought that should resound loudly in the minds of the readers is that what used to be known as Nazi Germany, has been out of the hands of the Nazis for over sixty years and yet remains the strongest bastion of racism and anti-Semitism of any developed nation. More people are beaten and killed in that part of the world for being Jewish, or Black than any other place with television and electricity.

Relative to Fidelity, the World's lessons end up teaching that true fidelity – life-lasting, unfailing, "until death do us part" type of fidelity – is unattainable and should not be expected or encouraged. I have heard "biblical" marriage counselors tell classes that if their spouse should fall short on the fidelity meter, that they should be forgiven, and all should move on into the future. And, while a transgression may warrant forgiveness, a pattern of behaviour would be something else. Still, when our culture gets to the presidential impeachment of William Jefferson Clinton, the culture chose to turn the other cheek, even though the man has a life-long pattern of marital infidelity, business impropriety, and ungodly policy. And even in view of that history of infidelity, the culture, as a whole, encouraged the marriage of the Clintons to continue, and the Presidency to remain "as is," and that the character flaws should be dismissed. I can't begin to tell you how many times I heard people say that Bill didn't do anything that every other man or woman hasn't done. But again, the research and surveys show us that every other man or woman hasn't done and won't do what Bill did.

By any standard Christian form and understanding of marital morality, Mrs. Clinton should have called it quits with Mr. Clinton after the second, or fourth or sixth "indiscretion." But indiscretion is hardly the right word for a long-standing and well documented habitual pattern of infidelity, is it? Still, since she is

51

aware (because the whole nation is aware) that he is philanderer of some noted accomplishment and she still chooses to stay with him, it must be an arrangement with which she is at least somewhat satisfied – or in which she gets something else that she needs. But is that what is primarily significant? Is the apparent satisfaction of a single partner all there is to be considered? If the one partner is happy cheating on his wife, and she has no problem turning the other cheek, is that a satisfactory arrangement? Is it a marriage? And, what about the other partner? What about God? And, please understand that I am not pointing fingers here, and I am not stating the right and wrong of it all. I am just raising the questions.

Please understand that the Clintons are just public examples of what has happened in thousands of households across America. Not that so many have a partner that is chronically unfaithful, but many have a single incident of failure in faithfulness. But, does the fact that some do have this moment of foolishness in their lives mean that this kind of failure should be expected for everyone else? Should it be considered a "given?" Should the failures of a few become the accepted standard by which the many are measured? Worse yet; should the expectation of failure be applied to the whole, not as a standard, but as an anticipated pinnacle or principle in what the whole have done or will do? Should all be assumed guilty of the same failure? Should it be assumed that guilt of failure is the pattern and the norm? Is failure an acceptable standard? The answer to all these questions is, "No!" Remember those surveys? Remember the thirty percent? Not only should failure not be accepted as a standard, it should not be expected at all. What should be expected is success. What should be encouraged is faith and faithfulness, not failure.

Remember that in a letter to the Corinthians (1 Corinthians 13), Paul says:

> 1 Corinthians 13:4-8 (NIV) "Love is patient, love is kind. It does not envy, it does not boast, it is not proud. It is not rude, it is not self-seeking, it is not easily angered, it keeps no record of wrongs. Love does not delight in evil but rejoices with the truth. It always protects, always trusts, always hopes, always perseveres. Love never fails. But where there are prophecies, they will cease; where there are tongues, they will be stilled; where there is knowledge, it will pass away."

Love always protects, and trusts, and hopes, and perseveres. Love never fails. The most amazing part of this passage is how incredibly true it continues to be. Love results in fidelity, and more. But fidelity is the subject of this part of the work.

In a scene from the recent movie *King Arthur* [13] the Romans have just frustrated the knights regarding a lifelong promise and are requiring they fulfill what may be a suicide mission. One of the knights says about their new orders on the day they were supposed to be released from their indenture, "The Romans have broken their word. We have the word of Arthur. That is enough!" When a people, who have just been betrayed by someone, are willing to trust another with their lives . . . this is the definition of "Fidelity." It is the kind of fidelity that seals the Declaration of Independence[14] in the words: "And for the support of this Declaration, with a firm reliance on the protection of divine Providence, we mutually pledge to each other our Lives, our Fortunes and our sacred Honor." And after this, fifty six men signed the document and in so doing put their lives and everything they owned at risk for the ideals of liberty and justice for all. Over two hundred and thirty years later, we can only understand a glimmer of what their idea of fidelity was and how important it can be.

Just another thought on fidelity; I believe that the person's sexuality belongs to their spouse. To some, this is a hard pill to swallow, even for those married for years, but what about those who are not yet married? When should the "spouse" rule be applied? I believe that it should be applied for life – from the beginning until the end. This means that when one is sixteen or twenty and single, and they have a sexual encounter with anyone other than their spouse, they have committed adultery. Now, I realize that adultery is a word that is seldom used anymore outside of a divorce court, or a Sonday School lesson on the Ten Commandments, but it is a very real concern. We can easily look back at the former President Clinton's philanderings and say with a pointed finger "that is adultery" – but it is hard to realize that it is no more or less sinful than a young couple who really believe that they are in love, losing their virginity to one another at prom.

No, I am not saying that there are no differences. After all, one is a first time occurrence with a slightly misguided, but still deeply caring motivation, while the other is an obviously selfish, repetitively blatant, and self motivated – as well as violating all manner of trust and care. And while their motivations and patterns are almost exact opposites, the sin is exactly the same. It really doesn't matter if you are cheating on a wife you have had for years or on a husband that you haven't even met, it is still the same cheating.

And it doesn't make a bit of difference if it is the man or woman whom you "plan" to marry. After all, no one can say for certain (without the gift of prophecy) what will happen in the future. Even if all the intentions are great, what if there is some heinous accident on the way to the ceremony and the wedding never happens? Then the wedding never happens! Bob and Rita are engaged, and in the heat of passion they consummate their relationship before they finalize with a wedding. It really doesn't matter if her father kills him for violating his daughter, or if he gets mugged and falls into a coma, or he already has a wife, or if he got what he really wanted from her and hits the road; the result is still a prematurely consummated no-wedding situation. This is infidelity.

Fidelity is Ronald Reagan having such a deep and abiding respect for the office of the Presidency, that everyone who knew him said that he couldn't even force himself to remove his suit coat in the oval office, much less his pants. Fidelity is John McCain being offered an early release from a Viet-Cong prison for political reasons and not taking it because there were others that were there before him that should be released first. Fidelity is John Kennedy – not with Marilyn – in the South Pacific giving his all to help keep his men alive in a dire situation.

"I will be with you always, even to the end of the age." That is Fidelity! Abraham takes his son Isaac to the top of Mount Moriah, and that is a picture of fidelity. Another example is in Revelation 22:5 (NASB) "And there will no longer be any night; and they will not have need of the light of a lamp nor the light of the sun, because the Lord God will illumine them; and they will reign forever and ever."

What is Love?

Contrary to common thought, love is not primarily a feeling. At least, not the love that makes the bond of marriage. In the case of marital love, the meaning runs much deeper and wider than any kind of feelings, and takes into account such things as surrender, devotion, commitment, and more. The idea of "love at first sight" is one that belittles love to its most simple and base forms. For the Christian to fall victim to the notion of "love at first sight," is to have bought into the Greco-Roman myth of the cherub that pierces your heart with his arrow to strike you with love. You may even hear vague references to this when someone says that someone has be hit by Cupid's arrow. Equally silly is the idea of "falling" into love, as if it were an accident that should have been avoided. The English language gets its primary problems with Love because it gets its linguistic understandings via the Romance languages, from Latin, which, although it may have 108 different forms of a single word and how to say it, there is one word for Love, and it is a verb. That verb, in all of its variations has been modified into a noun, adjective and adverb, and shoved into almost every application imaginable. "I love those curly fries." But if we are to understand Love as designed and defined by God, we should examine how God handles it in His Book.

In the Greek language of the New Testament there are several words for love. Let's check into it, eh? For the sake of this discourse we will keep the details limited. We are not interested in doing complex word studies here, and to be real honest, that has been done before, so what you are about to get are the "Cliff Notes[15]," so to speak – but not actually from the Cliff Notes people at all.

"Phileo" is that brotherly love which binds friends together. From that word the "City of Brotherly Love," Philadelphia, gets its name. It also encompasses the idea of caring for those within an association. This is the bond of a band, or a club, such as a fraternity. This one is pretty simple. It is the sense of caring for the neighbor and the guy in the next pew – and even the stranger in need on a roadside. Phileo does not necessarily require any personal attachment, or even prior knowledge to make it possible, though it does strengthen when those elements are involved. In its most basic form, phileo is what makes it possible for an unsaved soul to stop on the roadside and help a stranger with a flat in the rain. It is, in some small degree, the love of the brotherhood of man, or the brothers in your band or platoon.

The next to check out is "storgia," which means family affection – most commonly applied to the parent child relationship. Though not in the Bible, this is an attachment to someone whom you did not choose, but with whom the one has learned to appreciate and need the few or the many others. This is not only true within a family situation, but also in certain job situations where there is a bond such as soldiers, sailors, and marines. This is a love of others that is connected to a shared heritage, history, or experience, such as the same family tree, thousands of family dinners, common training, danger, and wartime.

The third on the list is "eros" – also not in the Bible – it is love as relates to sexual desire. It is an integral part of the puzzle that is marital love. It is also a part of the puzzle for extra-marital sex. It is, in fact, that attraction that one finds in another that has little to do with *who* they are, but more to do with *what* they are – physically. The word eros is the linguistic root of the words "erotic" and "erogenous." It is that sexual quality of attraction that can better be explained than it can be identified. It is easier in life to qualify it than to quantify it. That is because it depends on the excitement preferences in the individual. For example, one man likes women with larger bottoms, and another man, not so much. But the second man prefers a woman be a bit more "top-heavy" and likes voluptuous lips, while a third man likes thin-lipped women who are skinny from top to bottom. No one really knows why these preferences are what they are, although, there seems to be some attachment to the adults in our raising that we view as having positive influences – bringing good into our lives.

I knew a college professor that always wondered why he has such a personal predilection for women who were tall and sturdy. At least he wondered that when he was young. Later he realized that this was the body type of the grandmother who raised him. It wasn't that he was sexually attracted to his grandmother, but that he had a strong endearment and respect for the woman who endured hardships to raise him. So, deep inside his mind, he associated that particular body type with the character traits he wanted in a mate. For him, this association was pretty well engrained. For some men, the woman of their dreams is going to greatly resemble their mother or their favorite aunt, and for others the resemblance may not be that direct. It may be that their preferences are established by more than one woman or man. This was less prevalent in previous centuries, but dominant in recent history due to the bombardment of the senses with images of people in sensual settings and erotic posing, if only to sell jeans. Some of these preferences are established in our youth based on film image preferences of our parents, which would explain why so many men raised in the sixties like women shaped like Sophia Loren and Raquel Welch, instead of the skinny, shapeless women of the nineties and after. It also explains the screen success of such actresses as Angelina Jolie and Jessica Biel. Some are also going to conglomerate their preferences based on family, friends, and icons with images from movies and TV, including advertising. There is a lot of selling going on out there, and in reality, a child of ten has seen more people than my great-grandfather did in his entire life.

The final word for love is the most commonly used one in the New Testament, and that is "agape" (pronounced as: ah'-gah-pay). From a classical Greek literary point of view, it is almost exclusively reserved for the expression of the love of a god for a god. Until the events and the writing of the New Testament, the idea of agape being applied to us poor lowly humans, either as regards a deity loving humans, or humans loving someone (human or deity), or being loved by someone in the agape sense, was just about never done – never spoken, never written. People were seen as capable of storgia, eros, and phileo – but not agape. And for the most part, that may well be true. Agape is that unconditional love that is believed to come from the presence of God within the believer. In that way the believer can truly have the "love of God" in them, that love which is deific, which can be genuinely unconditional . . . agape. Because God resides within the believer, and God can love in this way, the believer becomes a conduit for God's love, loving unconditionally.

Christian marital love should really be a combination of all four of these forms of love. A husband and wife should be excellent friends (phileo), and they should be familial (storgia), they should be sexual (eros), and unconditional or deific (agape) in their love. And when we get all this together in one place and person, we realize that time has passed – and usually a lot more time has passed than we realize. When my wife and I stood up in a church to get married we really thought that we loved each other. Now, over a quarter century later, we realize what we didn't know very much about love at the time. And most importantly, we now know that we did not know very much about loving one another.

Do I believe in love at first sight? Not really. I believe in immediate attraction, immediate lust, instantaneous chemistry and such . . . but love? No. Love takes time and relationship and commitment. Love requires trust and faith and faithfulness. But right away . . . the scent of a woman, the right woman in a given moment, can fire a man up in a hurry. The right walk, shape, cleavage, bend, curve, and jiggle can be a man's complete undoing.

With these definitions of love in mind, I would like to quickly review the meeting of Jesus and Peter after the resurrection and Jesus is having a talk with Peter that goes like this:

> John 21:15-17 (NASB) So when they had finished breakfast, Jesus said to Simon Peter, "Simon, son of John, do you love Me more than these?" He said to Him, "Yes, Lord; You know that I love You." He said to him, "Tend My lambs."
>
> He said to him again a second time, "Simon, son of John, do you love Me?" He said to Him, "Yes, Lord; You know that I love You." He said to him, "Shepherd My sheep."
>
> He said to him the third time, "Simon, son of John, do you love Me?" Peter was grieved because He said to him the third time, "Do you love Me?" And he said to Him, "Lord, You know all things; You know that I love You." Jesus said to him, "Tend My sheep."

In this passage the English translation is "Jesus said to Simon Peter, "Simon, son of John, do you love Me more than these?" He said to Him, "Yes, Lord; You know that I love You." He said to him, "Tend My lambs."

But a more accurate understanding would be "Jesus said to Simon Peter, "Simon, son of John, do you agape Me more than these?" He said to Him, "Yeah,

Lord; You know that I phileo You." He said to him, "Tend My lambs." And this was said twice, until the third time, and that should really be read as: He said to him the third time, "Simon, son of John, do you phileo Me?" Peter was grieved because He said to him the third time, "Do you phileo Me?" And he said to Him, "Lord, You know all things; You know that I phileo You." Jesus said to him, "Tend My sheep."

This is how the translator sees the text.

For some reason Jesus changes the job offer from tending lambs, to shepherding sheep, to tending sheep, but if you are going to be given the job of providing spiritual nourishment to the adults of the flock, who will then pass on what they receive to the youth, you had better have their absolute best interests in heart. Also, a difference between "shepherding" and "tending" may be that the shepherd is a hireling, but the one who tends is an owner/keeper. I believe that this kind of dedication can only be had with complete, undeniable, unrelenting, and unconditional love that is from and truly by God. The Hebrew language is more of a brush-stroke and spray-can language as compared to Greek, which is more of a razor blade and scalpel sort of language. In Hebrew the word for love is 'ahab, and covers much of the meaning inferred by the English/American use of the word "love." It would not be used in the sense of loving your favorite cereal, or your best pair of shoes, or going to the mall, but everything else is there. Read this passage from The Song of Songs.

Song of Songs 8:5-7 (NIV)

Who is this coming up from the desert leaning on her lover?
Under the apple tree I roused you; there your mother
conceived you, there she who was in labor gave you birth.

Place me like a seal over your heart, like a seal on your arm;
for love is as strong as death, its jealousy unyielding as the
grave.
It burns like blazing fire, like a mighty flame.

Many waters cannot quench love; rivers cannot wash it
away.
If one were to give all the wealth of his house for love, it
would be utterly scorned.

In this passage the speaker reaches back into the past, to his lover's conception and birth to begin his odyssey of love and asks her to bond to him as he blazes with adoration for her in a flame that is unquenchable, un-washable and un-bribable. This is love.

And how about John 3:16? "For God so loved the world, that he gave his only begotten Son, that whosoever believeth in him should not perish, but have everlasting life." How many times have you seen on TV, or even in real life, a guy that won't even let his girlfriend take his car? Is it a big deal when a man gives his woman flowers, or jewelry? How much more does it display an amazing love when one is willing to give of himself, or of his family? Knowing that the price was going to be death, Jesus willingly became that sacrifice as the price of the bride. This opens up the discussion of another concept altogether; a bride price.

In an older world there is a tradition that goes back way beyond the idea of a dowry, and that is the concept of the bride price. It is the price demanded by the father of the bride, or offered by the potential groom. It may be paid in goats, camels, cattle, cash, or property. It is a gauge of how much the bride to be is valued within the community and of how dearly the groom, or groom's father, feels about the young woman. Also involved is the desire of the father to keep the girl at home, counterbalanced by how much her bride price could help the family, and more importantly, how much good for the daughter the father feels he can do by marrying her off to the best choice groom he thinks he can possibly find and negotiate for her. If the bride is wealthy, well loved by her father, and living in a large community, then a small price would not get his attention and induce him to part with his daughter. If the father is poor and the family needy, if the community is small and remote, and the economy is depressed, a goat may do, as it would provide milk for the family for its lifetime. In the case of Jesus being the payment, there is no higher price that could be paid for the bride. What father pays His only Son? Consider that in the Church/Bride arrangement, the guardian of the Bride is the same father of the groom, and then realize that he already owns everything that is, anywhere and anytime. What price can be paid to one so wealthy as to own absolutely everything already?

I heard a sermon once by a pastor whose thesis was that, as our relationship becomes deeper with the Lord, we become more valuable. He related it to the relationships of people, wherein two people become closer and consequentially, become more important to one another. And I paid full attention to his words and expressions; he was telling the congregation that if they would grow in faith and relationship, that they would be more valuable to God. But what he failed to realize is that the value of a person is established back in Genesis 9:6 (NIV) "Whoever sheds the blood of man, by man shall his blood be shed; for in the image of God has God made man." The value of a man is in whose image he is made, not in the matter by which he is made. His chemical value seems to change from time to time, and may, one day, top a hundred bucks, but the value of the man is really in whose image he is made.

Jesus asks, "Whose image is stamped on these coins?" That conversation ends in, "Give unto Caesar what is Caesar's, and give to the Lord what is the Lord's." As the coin is made in the image of Caesar, so you and I are made in the image of God. In the same thought we find both our value and our debt. For if we truly do love God, who has paid the greatest and gravest price for us, should we not pay our debt with that into which His image is pressed? So the price for saving me, is me? Very interesting.

If the value of a person is in the fact that we are each made in the image of God, I suggest that the price associated with that value is defined in the fact that Jesus Messiah would pay his own life to save even only one of us from eternal

58

death. You are important and valuable beyond measure, and there is nothing you can do to make that value greater or smaller. Except for Sons of Belial.

Matrimony

Matrimony is something that is viewed by different people in different ways. In the Anglo-American cultures, we tend to view marriage in pretty much the same way. In fact, the Merriam-Webster Dictionary[16] at http://www.m-w.com defines matrimony as:

Main Entry: mat·ri·mo·ny
Function: *noun*
Etymology: Middle English, from Middle French
matremoine, from Latin *matrimonium*, from *matr-*, *mater*
mother, matron -- more at MOTHER
the union of man and woman as husband and wife :
MARRIAGE

Within the Church it is usually referred to as "Holy Matrimony" because the union itself is supposed to be either initiated by God or incorporating God in the contract of human matrimony. By that standard, and with God being either the initiator or a partner, this is a Holy arrangement. I think both are true. I believe that God is the initiator, in that it is He who made the arrangement from its very beginning. Also, I believe that it is God who initiates legitimate individual marriages. I add the word "legitimate" as a caveat because there are illegitimate marriages as well.

I know a pastor who "fell in love" with an executive assistant/ choir director, become deeply committed to that person and together decide that it is God's will that they should marry. The thing that makes all of this illegitimate is that they are each already married to someone else. So, they divorce and re-marry, claiming that it is God's will. I mention the pastor because I want all to understand that even those in leadership, those with lots of training in God's Word, those who should profoundly know better, can get caught up in their own desires and find excuses for what they want, far and away, above and beyond what they know God has made clear, and even credit (or blame) God for it. It has been going on for a very long time. Remember, Adam said, "It was THAT WOMAN, that YOU gave me" – wanting to place blame on Eve, and then redirecting his blame on God, instead of owning up to his own actions and taking responsibility. The great comic, and esteemed theologian, Rabbi Red Buttons once pointed out that Adam could have NOT taken the fruit and said to God, "I got more ribs; you got more broads?"

But that is not the way we work, is it? That is not the way we think. We wrestle and angle and finagle to try to find ways to make God's Word fit our will. It has been said by many scholars and teachers, as well as critics and anti-Christians, that a person can make the Bible say just about anything that he or she wants of it. But, I contend, he or she cannot do so honestly. This is why I am a stickler for learning to treat the Word with integrity as early as possible. And I am a fervent believer in building up an intelligent and profound reverence for it that shames the nay-sayers. After all, if one goes to a liberal seminary and is taught that the Word is either less than it is, or that it doesn't mean what it seems to say, it becomes easier to "decide" what it says than to discover what it says. And, let's face it, when we decide what it says, it almost always says what we want to hear. Just as an example, Paul says that we are no longer under the Law (Romans 6:14), does that give us license to ignore the Law in any way? Paul says, Romans 3:31 (NASB) "Do we then nullify the Law through faith? May it never be! On the contrary, we establish the Law." Paul is saying that the Law is ratified in our faith so that we can now have power to live more agreeably within the Law – not under its condemnation for our guilt – but according to its demands. Does that mean that we can uphold all 613 laws? No, but we can always do better, and growing in grace, do better and better.

Getting back to the illegitimate marriages above, if God has given a universal instruction "thou shall not covet thy neighbor's wife," being Born Again and not "under the Law" does not release anyone from that command. The only possible thing that could release someone from that command would be a direct intervention by God, so they assume that this must be what has happened – that God has brought them together and therefore it is a union that He not only approves, but has, in fact, designed and desires. After all, aren't they special in God's eyes? Don't they merit some sort of special treatment? But I read somewhere that God is no respecter of persons (Lev 19:15; Deut 1:17; 16:19; Ps 82:2, Prov 17:15, 18:5, 24:23, 28:21) and He doesn't make special rules for some above others. Just a thought, but if He did not make special rules for David, why should He make special rules for you or me? And besides, if God had directly intervened for these two married people to marry; wouldn't their previous spouses be deceased or otherwise removed from the picture?

In the case of the pastor mentioned above, as in many cases every day, the fidelity of their Holy Matrimonies has been betrayed, but neither fidelity nor matrimony has failed – only a couple of the participants. And sometimes, those who do the cheating – do the misleading of the congregations – aren't even aware (blinded by their own desires) that they are cheating and misleading. Paul warned:

> Acts 20:27-31 NIV "For, I have not hesitated to proclaim to you the whole will of God. Keep watch over yourselves and all the flock of which the Holy Spirit has made you overseers. Be shepherds of the church of God, which he bought with his own blood. I know that after I leave, savage wolves will come in among you and will not spare the flock. Even from your own number men will arise and distort the truth in order to draw away disciples after them. So be on your guard! Remember that for three years I never stopped warning each of you night and day with tears."

When Paul says that "even from your own number men will arise," he is speaking to a group of what he considers faithful men – elsewise he would have removed the ones in question personally. He trusts them, just as you and I trust our friends and neighbors, teachers and leaders – and that is as it should be. But people change. Sometimes they change for the good, sometimes for bad, and sometimes they just change into something different – neither better nor worse; just different. And this is true in marriage as well.

The goal in marriage is to be together – in agreement – when change occurs, and that is why Holy Matrimony is a bond making two people into "one flesh." And since it is Holy Matrimony, meaning that God is a part of it, the change should always be toward the better, stronger, holier. Realistically speaking, doesn't God enter each of our lives with a desire to making it a better life – doing a better job at everything – being a better person, husband, wife, friend, etc. – so as to bring glory to Himself? Is there any among us who can honestly say that they believe that God got into their life to make it worse? I believe that all would agree that this is foolishness. As Paul would say, "May it never be!" (Ro 3:4, Ro 3:6, Ro 3:31, Ro 6:2, Ro 6:15, Ro 7:7, Ro 7:13, Ro 9:14, Ro 11:1, Ro 11:11, Gal 2:17, Gal 3:21, Gal 6:14, 1 Cor 6:15,)

Matrimony is fidelity. It is Holy because God is part and partner of it. It is a bond bringing people together to make a union of one flesh, intended to become better than it could be without the other parties. It is a lifelong agreement, in that it is designed and intended to last until death – not to be broken by either party involved or anyone outside the contract. But, is it monogamous?

Monogamy

The question that I wish to address is not whether your marriage or mine is monogamous, but whether that is the only design and intent. Again, I would like to emphasize that we are not interested in what is social opinion, or cultural bias, or even what our personal proclivities may be. We are here to explore what is the perfect and permissive will or desire of God – not you, me, and the local congregation, or the pope – but of God. That being said, let's take a look in the Word.

The first appearance of polygyny is in Genesis 4:19-24 (NASB)

Lamech took to himself two wives: the name of the one was
    Adah, and the name of the other, Zillah.
Adah gave birth to Jabal; he was the father of those who
    dwell in tents and have livestock. His brother's
    name was Jubal; he was the father of all those who
    play the lyre and pipe.
As for Zillah, she also gave birth to Tubal-cain, the forger of
    all implements of bronze and iron; and the sister of
    Tubal-cain was Naamah.

Lamech said to his wives, "Adah and Zillah, Listen to my
voice, You wives of Lamech, Give heed to my
speech, For I have killed a man for wounding me;
And a boy for striking me; If Cain is avenged
sevenfold, Then Lamech seventy-sevenfold."

It is assumed by many preachers and teachers that, because the passage speaks so profoundly of Lamech's arrogance, that having two wives was a part of his sinful nature. And that may or may not be.

Lamech "took" to himself two wives. It is unclear as to the intent of this, except that he "had" two wives. Usually today, when a man has two wives, or more, it is considered Bigamy or Polygamy, and it usually results from a covert arrangement whereby the wives may not know about one another, or by which they are forced into the arrangement. In the practice of Polygyny there is a single family, or in some definitions a single marriage, in which multiple wives participate. There is a difference that needs to be understood, and which will be addressed in a future treatise.

For Lamech, it may be that he literally "took" his wives by force, which seems to be a part of his modus operandi as a man of force, but he is revealing that he is setting himself above common and acceptable actions. It may be that multiple wives were common at the time, and the reference here is to his use of force to get them. It may be that it is just an expression of his self-esteem being so great as to poise himself above the statements of God about Cain for his protection. If this is a statement that is just about Lamech's sinful nature, the Bible has many examples of God appeasing man's sinful nature without actually sinning. As such, isn't having one wife also appeasing to our sinful nature? Paul would rather that we all be single, like him, but that it is better to marry than to burn. Hmm!

Sexual desires are considered by many as reflective of our sinful nature, but fulfilling those sexual desires inside the context of marriage is not sin. As further evidence, God does not prohibit certain things in a codified Law until such time has passed that this codification becomes reasonable. An example of this is the modern understanding of incest prohibiting even the marriage of siblings or step-siblings. This prohibition surely extends to half-siblings (having one parent in common), yet Cain was almost certainly bound to his sister and Abraham was definitely married to his half-sister. Abraham and Sarai had the same Father and different mothers (Genesis 20:12). And even that begs the question of whether Abraham's father, Terah had multiple wives or if he was widowed. We have no evidence to suggest an answer.

But we do have other evidence that should be discussed. We should look at David and Solomon and their harems of wives and concubines. We should also discuss briefly what are a wife and a concubine.

Understand that the word concubine, in the biblical sense, is not the same as in the oriental sense. In the Orient (north and east of India), the concubine is often property of a man for the purposes of pleasure, companionship, and comfort. In the Turkish and Arab world, she is called an odalisque. She lives to serve and in the most traditional, cultural understanding, her offspring are also property of the man, not to be considered as his children at all.

In the biblical sense, the concubine is a wife without a share of inheritance. She has all the same rights of conjugality, welfare, and provision, but not a share of inheritance. It is as though they were employing the legal technology that we now call a pre-nuptial agreement. If she is a concubine she cannot be dismissed by a wife, even after the husband's death. She is usually provided for in such a way as to assure a happy life, so to speak. She may be given a piece of land and/or a monetary provision of some sort, which she and/or her children will have to manage like any widow in modern America would do. What she is left, with her children, would be like a "cash settlement" or a particular property. And here is the difference. If the man dies the concubine should be left what is mentioned above, but the wives and their children are left his corporate holdings, his social position, as well as any political power, and this is left in shares or fixed amounts and items. So that before David dies, it is Solomon, the son of a wife that is chosen as co-regent with David in his old age, and Solomon becomes King after David's death. If Bathsheba had been a concubine, this choice would not have been possible at all. When Solomon dies, the son that takes his place is also not the son of a concubine, because a concubine has no legal right to inheritance, and neither do her children. A wife could be willed a portion (percentage) or an item or an amount.

A similar situation arose when Howard Hughes died and his "heirs" began trying to divvy up his holdings. The relatives began coming out of the woodwork like cockroaches, each seeking their slice of Howard's earnings and enterprises. But, in the last known will there is said to have been a clause that some guy who had given Howard a ride, a meal, and rest when he was ragged, tired, hungry, and hitchhiking was (allegedly) left a couple of hundred thousand dollars. Now, this gent's receipts from Howard were in fact limited to the exact amount Howard stated in his will – but on the other hand, it went to him FIRST, and afterward . . . the cockroaches.

Now, most of what we may call "New Testament People" will say that multiple wives is no longer acceptable, and I would argue that they are just as right as they are wrong, and here is why. In their defense they would usually cite two passages 1Timothy 3:1-4 and Titus 1:5-7 as imposing the single wife rule. See the passages here.

> 1 Timothy 3:1-4 (NASB)It is a trustworthy statement: if any man aspires to the office of overseer, it is a fine work he desires to do. An overseer, then, must be above reproach, the husband of one wife, temperate, prudent, respectable, hospitable, able to teach, not addicted to wine or pugnacious, but gentle, peaceable, free from the love of money. He must be one who manages his own household well, keeping his children under control with all dignity

Titus 1:5-7 (NASB) For this reason I left you in Crete, that you would set in order what remains and appoint elders in every city as I directed you, namely, if any man is above reproach, the husband of one wife, having children who believe, not accused of dissipation or rebellion. For the overseer must be above reproach as God's steward, not self-willed, not quick-tempered, not addicted to wine, not pugnacious, not fond of sordid gain,

A few things should be noted before really getting into those two passages as "proof texts" and the first thing is that it is regarding the choice of what are called Elders and Bishops. Regardless of what else may be considered, the fact is that they are proposing the one wife imposition on people who are to be selected for church office of some sort. Regardless of how one positions Deacons, Elders, Bishops, etc, they are all positions of authority within the congregation – and positions that are desired, chosen, or selected. Further, they are purposely recognized positions – as Paul says, "that you would set in order what remains and appoint elders" (Titus 1:5) – which are a part of setting things in order.

There may be a few that insist that we should all desire to be leaders of such note, or that we should at least live as such examples to the world, but the reality is that Paul did not see that as a standard for all, and neither did God. Paul did see the standard to abstain from food sacrificed to idols, from blood, from the meat of strangled animals and from sexual immorality – as agreed in the Council of Jerusalem in Acts 15, and there are lists of people (identities) that will be denied access to the Kingdom – such as idolaters and fornicators and homosexuals and more – but monogamy was imposed on only the leadership, and apparently only on the leadership of certain areas, cities, regions or territories. It really only mentions it in the land that is the heart and soul of Hellenism.

Another reality is that this was written to people in a different culture from Paul's own Jewish raising – far from the Middle East. It was a land that accepted slavery, homosexuality, and temple prostitutes, and Paul was setting a standard for the church leaders of the time, and in that place, to be so far above the standard of the culture that they would never fall under sexual or marital aspersion or disrespect in those communities. In a culture where slavery was acceptable and sexual immorality was "not so bad," monogamy would be viewed as the most impressive of social and cultural standards. One of the social truths of life is that, even if people don't publicly care for the highly moral people of the world, they secretly admire them if they actually keep to their high moral code, live out their Law in life and don't try to impose their rules on others . . . other than by example. An excellent example of this is Ed Begley, Jr. There are thousands of environmentalist actors and pundits in the world, but Ed and his family live their faith. I don't agree with their environmental conclusions but I respect him immensely, because of his commitment by his actions not his words. Also, he doesn't tend to tell the rest of us that we have to do it his way.

In the Gospels we see a people that are called God-fearers, who are attracted to the Jewish ways, though not fully converted. And a common reason is because they see, in the Jewish culture and families, a life that they admire. They are drawn in by the fact that the Jewish life is so ordered, caring, and fulfilled. This is sometimes enough to attract the common man or woman, and Paul knows it, so he says that the leadership should show it. Paul wants the leaders of the church to be of such a high social caliber that no one has anything disrespectful to say about them. They are to be the same kind of beacon of fulfilled and caring order that Judaism has been to the world, even still today. It is also no different from when he commands that women keep their hair long and men keep their hair short. It is a cultural thing that makes a statement in the immediate surroundings that may not resonate elsewhere.

Likewise, in the case of David and Solomon – the two most extreme examples – having multiple wives is not considered a sin. When David takes Bathsheba, the sin he has committed is not of attaining another wife, but of taking the wife of another man, and then killing her husband. In fact, God addresses him in this matter, through Nathan, and says, "I also gave you your master's house and your master's wives into your care, and I gave you the house of Israel and Judah; and if that had been too little, I would have added to you many more things like these!" (2 Samuel 12:8 NASB) If God were concerned with the idea of David having too many wives, He would have said so. But what He said was, "I would have added to you many more things like these," if David did not have enough. Now, that does not seem to express any thought that the number of wives was a problem, but rather that the choice and means of getting Bathsheba was a problem.

David is said to have had about three hundred wives and concubines and for Solomon that number was at about one thousand, and even those excessive numbers were not considered or mentioned by God as polygamous sin. Though Solomon's wives "led him astray," David's did not. Do we conclude that the magic number of wives falls somewhere between 300 and 1000? Or do we conclude that our heart should still follow after Yahweh, regardless of spousal attachments, many, few, one, or none?

There is a note or two in Leviticus about avoiding certain polygamous situations. For example, one should not marry a woman AND her sister it is called "wickedness" (Leviticus 18:17 NIV) and he is not to marry a woman AND her sister (while she is alive). He is also not to enter into sexual relations with his father's wife (without regard to whether she is his mother), his own sister (whether full, half, or step) and he should avoid such with his aunt or niece. But, just the fact that the man is admonished to not take specific women as additional wives; it is also a strong indication that additional wives, as a whole, are not unacceptable.

Why not additional husbands? One should address this question before every N.O.W.[17] member in the universe begins chanting. Simply put, it is a matter of traceable blood and traceable inheritance, family tree. By inheritance we don't mean just property and money, but also social, political, religious, and physical traits. For starters, we are to assume that the marital union is undefiled by interlopers when making accounts of the inheritances, but consider what the situation is when a woman has more than one husband and a child is born. Whose blood and medical history does that child share? Further, if the father is a part of a given tribe of Native American – as regards casino shares, or descended from a particular tribe of Israel – regarding royalty or priesthood, or any other unforeseen circumstances of heritage, there may be remunerations or responsibilities that could never be known in advance.

Today we can determine actual parentage with a DNA test, but should we have to? And what of those born in the previous 5000 years? Additionally, multiple men in a house tend to be time-bombs awaiting explosion. And, in the final analysis, who would then be the head of the house? While that may seem an archaic concept for some people, it is a valid one.

There should be a head of household, and regardless of who earns the most money, has the best job, is primary caregiver to the kids, or whatever, it is ordained by God that the man should bear the greatest responsibility and authority. And before the aforementioned N.O.W. members chanting begins again, remember that God asks the submission of the woman to the man, and he asks the total self-sacrifice of the man for the woman. Who really has the better end of that deal?

Now comes the "catch" if you will. The catch is that what God allows and what God commands are different things. We rely on a principle laid down by the Apostles in Acts 4:19 (NASB) "But Peter and John answered and said to them, 'Whether it is right in the sight of God to give heed to you rather than to God, you be the judge.'" The principle plays out as this: If God commands that we do something that is contrary to the laws of men then we obey God. But the converse is also true, in that, if the law of man forbids something and God allows it, but does not command, then it is forbidden for the Christian to take what God allows – because it is unlawful in the eyes of man. We are called to obey the laws of man as long as they do not fly in the face of the laws of God. It's kind of like that gum-chewing business from before.

In the "Fundamentalist Latter Day Saints" (a division of Mormonism) they teach a thing they call "The Principle," whereby a man must take multiple wives in order to be obedient to the command to be fruitful and multiply, but if they are looking to become gods over their own planets some day, they have to have enough wives and enough children to run the place. This is a perversion that keeps so many deceived in so many ways that I may someday have to write a book about this one error.

But, if you are an American Christian, then it is likely that you will have a "One Wife at a Time" kind of matrimony; subject to the changes in American law, and/or modification of your marital agreement with your spouse. If you are an Eastern/Asian or Arab Christian, however, it may be fully acceptable for you to have multiple wives. Much of this is going to be as cultural as the matter of the haircut to Paul, who, as a Rabbi would have had flowing locks, even though he taught the Corinthians to cut the hair on the men and grow the hair of the women.

Regarding the culturalization of our understanding of matrimony, be aware that in a study running from 1960 to 1980, called the *Ethnographic Atlas*,[18] of 1,231 societies noted, 186 were monogamous; 453 had occasional polygyny; 588 had more frequent polygyny; and 4 had polyandry. This is an interesting collection of figures, not because it spans an extensive period of time (20 years:

1960-1980), but because it is recent – some might say, almost current. It shows that our American understanding of Marriage – one man/one woman – is not the most prevalent, popular or even profound. Monogamy is considered as the norm in America, but in reality, globally, and historically, it has not been the standard by which the world exists.

Not only does Polygyny – the marriage with one man and multiple wives – still remain in myriad locations today, it existed in the Reformation days, was discussed and debated, and the decision of many of the great thinkers for the faith did not come to the same conclusions as most modern American pastors. So, before we accept the word of someone saying, "This has never been acceptable!" Maybe we should look at what some of the great thinkers had to say on the matter, so sit back and relax – or not.

When asked by Henry VIII about his lack of an heir, presumably due to his barren wife, Martin Luther told him that – to marry Anne Boleyn as well, without killing Catherine of Aragon would be the lesser evil. Now, agreeably, we do not usually come to grips with theology by what is the lesser evil. This is not the matter of Rahab having to choose between lying and allowing the death of the hiding Hebrews. This is a matter of choices whereby Henry could have chosen "none of the above," which was not an option for Rahab. But if he wanted an heir, and all kings want heirs – most men for that matter – then he had to get a replacement from somewhere, by some means. Martin Luther later wrote in a letter to the Saxon Chancellor Gregor Brück, "I confess that I cannot forbid a person to marry several wives, for it does not contradict the Scripture. If a man wishes to marry more than one wife he should be asked whether he is satisfied in his conscience that he may do so in accordance with the word of God. In such a case the civil authority has nothing to do in the matter." I am particularly enamored with the idea that "civil authority has nothing to do in the matter." Martin argued that government should have no rule or management of marriage at all; even by homosexuals, and even by polygynists.

The great theologian Philipp Melanchthon likewise counseled that Henry VIII need "not risk schism by dissolving his union with the established churches to grant himself divorces in order to replace his barren wives, but could instead look to polygamy as a suitable alternative."

The Lutheran pastor Johann Lyser (1631-1684) was imprisoned, beaten, and exiled from Italy to Holland because he so strongly defended polygyny in a work entitled *Polygamia Triumphatrix*, which he wrote under the pseudonym of "Theophilus."

Anabaptist leader Bernhard Rothmann (c. 1495 – c. 1535) eventually took nine wives, saying "God has restored the true practice of holy matrimony amongst us." as told by Carter Lindberg in "The European Reformations Sourcebook."[19]

Franz von Waldeck and others, accused Anabaptist leader John of Leiden of keeping 16 wives, and publicly beheading one when she disobeyed him. This was used as the basis for their conquest of Münster in 1535, according to Karl Kautsky's *"Communism in Central Europe at the Time of the Reformation."*[20] By the way, I don't recommend the beheading of any wife, regardless of the disobedience or disloyalty.

Lambeth Conferences of the Anglican Church are held about once every ten years, beginning in 1867. In 1888 they took up several subjects to discuss, one of which was plural marriage. In the conferences that took place until a recent one in 2008, they seem to have held several different positions, including in 1988 where they recommended that in places where "Churches face problems of polygamy" they are encouraged to share information regarding their pastoral approach "to Christians who become polygamists so that the most appropriate way of disciplining and pastoring them can be found." In 2008, according to their Resolution 114, the official position became "In the case of polygamy, there is a universal standard – it is understood to be a sin, therefore polygamists are not admitted to positions of leadership including Holy Orders, nor after acceptance of the Gospel can a convert take another wife, nor, in some areas, are they admitted to Holy Communion." Notice though, that the convert is not required to give up his numerous wives in order to become a Christian, or to remain a member of the Church, or church, in good standing. How many of you were taken by the part where it says "nor, in some areas, are they admitted to Holy Communion," as an example of consistent doctrine in all instances? Isn't that the same as saying that sin is geographical in nature? Hmm.

The Lutheran Church of Liberia *began* allowing multiple wives in the 1970's – those crazy Lutherans, eh? My own Great-X5-Grandfather, Johann Michael Krieger was married on June 24, 1764, in a Lutheran Church in Frederich, MD, to Catherine Mary David . . . and coincidentally, on the same date to Susanna Cullup; quite possibly at the same time. Understand that polygyny was not illegal in the US – by law – until shortly before the Civil War, and then it was only out of reaction to the Mormon conundrum and the public outcry against them. It was not officially criminalized and acted upon – in practice – until after the Civil War. Lincoln sent messages to Utah that, if they stayed out of the war, as a whole, he would defer any prosecution of polygamy of any kind. On January 4, 1896 Utah became a state, only after having succumbed to the pressure to ban polygamy. Hmm. By the way, Grandpa Johann's sin, from a Jewish perspective, is not that he married two women – been done before – but that he did not allow for a bridal week for the first wife, then another for the second, as were enjoyed by Leah and Rachel. Then again, they had been living in sin for many years when they tied the knot of knots.

More modernly, I ruminate upon the considerations of Rabbi Chaim Gruber, who speculates that the underlying reason why the Torah allows a man more than one wife at a time, while a woman is permitted only one husband at a time is biological. He posits that because a man may simultaneously father children with more than one woman, but it is highly improbable for a woman to become simultaneously pregnant by more than one man, that there is a biological parameter established. Therefore, as "marriage," in a strict or broad sense, means a joining together, as the genes of a man can simultaneously be joined together with the genes of multiple women via different conceptions, a man, can be married to more than one woman at once. A woman, however, is not naturally so joined to more than one man at a time. Presuming upon his premise of marriage as a joining of genes, it is notable that two men cannot join genes, and neither can two women.

With this joining of the genes considered, Rabbi Gruber states that the intent of the allowance of polygamy is "not to say that monogamous marriage isn't ideal," but rather to create a social construct which is inclusive of a common cultural phenomenon; "…as a man may be linked to several women at once, it is better to consider these multiple relationships legit, than to criminalize them and put them outside the bounds of normality. Doing so would wrongly shame many as 'living in sin,' and also unjustly condemn countless kids as 'bastards'." As many men have had children outside of their marriages, being able to marry the mothers of those children would legitimize those births, and legitimize those women as wives, instead of whatever else the culture may call them.

Chapter 5 – Keeping it Kosher

The first thing that must be understood is what it means to Keep Kosher. The hard part to wrap one's head around is the fact that most Christians and Jews cannot begin to define it to within a reasonably pointed agreement. As an expression in common conversation it implies that everything is honest, or gives the impression of being legitimate. It literally means to be in accordance with the Law. And, by the Law, we mean the Law of God as predominately prescribed in the books of Leviticus and Deuteronomy, but also in agreement with the principles presented throughout the Torah – Genesis through Deuteronomy.

Definition?

Specifically, something is Kosher if it is in agreement with the 613 laws handed down to Moses in the Judaic Law. In the scope of what is believed or accepted by the use of that term, we begin at what is truly the least Kosher and most common Christian belief; that if you love your neighbor, you have kept the law, therefore, you have kept Kosher. This is a severely flawed – but commonly accepted – variation of Jesus' words when asked about the Greatest Commandment:

> Matthew 22:36-40 (NIV) "Teacher, which is the greatest commandment in the Law?"
> Jesus replied: "'Love the Lord your God with all your heart and with all your soul and with all your mind.' This is the first and greatest commandment. And the second is like it: 'Love your neighbor as yourself.' All the Law and the Prophets hang on these two commandments."

The common Christian understanding of this is that if one does these two things, the rest is superfluous. In reality though, if one does truly keep to Loving God and Loving Neighbor, then he will in fact *do* the others to the best of his ability. As a paraphrase of James might say, "Show me your Faith *by* your Works." After all, if you truly love God, won't you learn His Law, so that you may do His Will, and His Love can be reflected in how you love you neighbor, fully in accordance with the Love and Will and Word of God?

John reminds us:

I John 3:23-24 (NASB) This is His commandment, that we believe in the name of His Son Jesus Christ, and love one another, just as He commanded us.
The one who keeps His commandments abides in Him, and He in him. We know by this that He abides in us, by the Spirit whom He has given us.

But one cannot keep "His commandments" if one ignores the Law, which is also His eternal commandment. If you hold to the divinity of Christ, then the same voice that says, "Seek ye first" also says, "Thou shalt not."

On the other end of the spectrum we find the most severely Orthodox of Jews hold to the idea that the standard is much higher, and even must be kept, not only in accord with the Law, but with the Mishna and Talmudic interpretation of what the Law means in its every phrase. Part of this idea comes from what is called the Oral Tradition, which is said to have been handed down throughout the generations, through priests and rabbis of all times, and partially codified into the Talmud, the Mishna, and the libraries of the remote locations of the Jewish world.

In the first example of the examination, the typical Christian says something that comes off as if 'not needing the Law,' and the most common saying is that to fail in any of the Law is to fail in all of the Law. But is that not the same as to say that we should not even try to behave? And, if we are actually expected to try to behave, by whose standard are we to measure our behaviour? Yours, mine . . . or God's?

I believe that the Heavens and Earth, and all creatures in each of them, were created by a Loving, Creative, Beneficent God, who has a personal interest in each and every one of us. Further, I believe that it is logical and reasonable to expect that God has a Creator's right to the standard of keeping for his creation. Just as an underwear company has a right to put a label in the waistband of the boxers telling you "no bleach, use warm wash/cool rinse, warm iron if needed"; God has the right to provide the best set of instructions for our keeping. Note also that the instructions in the tag of the underwear are for the best keeping of the garments. Not only does He have a Right, but He also has the wisdom to know the best possible set of instructions . . . for care and maintenance. He even has a responsibility to make the instructions knowable, manageable, and useable. The disagreement usually comes in the varying ideas of what these instructions are, whether simply guidelines or viable holy commands, and where to draw the lines as to what you are willing to accept within the realm of obedience, and what is beyond.

Examples – one way . . . then another:

In one passage of the Bible we are told not to soak the meat of the kid in the milk of the mother. According to the Talmud this begins with the direct combination of the milk of the Mother and the meat of the Kid (Exodus 23:19), but extends through human interdiction on the Law to say that one should either eat meat or dairy, but not both on the same day. This automatically rules out both

71

cheeseburgers and pizza in most forms. It also means that you can't eat a (beef) bologna sandwich and wash it down with a glass of milk.

On the other end of this discussion there are Christians who cite Peter's vision on the roof of Simon the Tanner (Acts 10:9-16) as defining an acceptable diet.

> Acts 10:9-16 (NIV) About noon the following day as they were on their journey and approaching the city, Peter went up on the roof to pray. He became hungry and wanted something to eat, and while the meal was being prepared, he fell into a trance. He saw heaven opened and something like a large sheet being let down to earth by its four corners. It contained all kinds of four-footed animals, as well as reptiles of the earth and birds of the air. Then a voice told him, "Get up, Peter. Kill and eat."
> "Surely not, Lord!" Peter replied. "I have never eaten anything impure or unclean."
> The voice spoke to him a second time, "Do not call anything impure that God has made clean."
> This happened three times, and immediately the sheet was taken back to heaven.

What they may fail to realize though is that the vision really isn't about food at all, but rather about a presumed "unclean" household that Peter is soon to visit. Two other points to recall, even if one cannot get past the idea that food is not the subject . . . *One*, that Peter does not eat any of it, and *Two*, God does not require that he eat anything before removing the sheet from him. Later, Peter offers explanation in this way:

> Acts 10:27-29 (NIV) Talking with him, Peter went inside and found a large gathering of people. He said to them: "You are well aware that it is against our law [tradition] for a Jew to associate with a Gentile or visit him. But God has shown me that I should not call any man impure or unclean. So when I was sent for, I came without raising any objection. May I ask why you sent for me?"

But most Christians pass by the explanation and the record of Peter not eating, and assume that this passage is about food and diet. And in these assumptions, they believe that anything is food except one another.

The closest passage to accomplishing their goal of an open diet is Mark 7:17-19 (NIV).

> After he had left the crowd and entered the house, his disciples asked him about this parable. "Are you so dull?" he asked. "Don't you see that nothing that enters a man from the

outside can make him 'unclean'? For it doesn't go into his heart but into his stomach, and then out of his body." (In saying this, Jesus declared all foods "clean.")

But, as often there may be, there is a catch. You see the part in parentheses, where it says, "(In saying this, Jesus declared all foods 'clean.')?" This is terribly translated. For a direct, linear translation, without additions or subtractions, take a look at this.

Mark 7:19 (NA27 Int.)

ὅτι οὐκ εἰσπορεύεται αὐτοῦ εἰς τὴν καρδίαν ἀλλ' εἰς τὴν κοιλίαν, καὶ εἰς τὸν ἀφεδρῶνα ἐκπορεύεται, καθαρίζων πάντα τὰ βρώματα

Mark 7:19 Paul R. McReynolds, "A Greek English Inter-Linear New Testament"

because not it travels in him into the heart but into the stomach and into the latrine it travels out cleaning all the foods

Read in context, it is not some great statement of Theological Doctrine about Hygiene Codes, it is, in fact, humor. Notice that a prominent item missing in the original language is that whole parenthetical part about, "*in saying this, Jesus declared*." It simply isn't in the text, but the humor remains. Remember that the discussion is about ritual hand washing, not pork rinds. Also remember that in using the word "unclean" we are discussing its ritual or ceremonial state, not general hygiene as understood by modern people and science. Once waste from the body is disposed of in the "latrine" it is not ceremonially unclean. It may be un-hygienic, but it is not "unclean." People who worked in sewage operations or latrine duty were not excluded from entering the Temple grounds or attending Synagogue, but someone who had handled road kill, a found dead thing, or a human body was unclean; this remained until they had (Lev 11:24, 25, 27, 31, 32) properly washed and the sun had gone down.

As a translational note, although the part where it says that "Jesus declared all foods clean" does not appear in any of the early manuscripts, it appears in dozens of modern translations, even though Jesus never said it, and Mark never wrote it, the modern Church still reads it. There are several other passages that are in the same category. Among the most prominent of those also not in eldest manuscripts is the "Woman caught in adultery" at John 8:3-11, and John 5:3e-4 about waiting for angels to stir the waters of the pool. These passages were actually added in long after the writers were dead.

Also, the problem the Pharisees and scribes were addressing, in the Mark 7 passage, was the oral tradition's teaching that a demon was hanging around your fingers and had to be rinsed off or it would be ingested, where it could overtake

73

someone. The more accurate translation may be, "because it doesn't enter the heart, but in the stomach, and out in the latrine where everything is clean." The humor only comes when you have a cultural understanding of something so distasteful as sewage as NOT being unclean. In handling this matter with humor, in this off handed way, he dismisses the traditions of the hoity-toity, for the honest realities of the hoi polloi. But there is more to it than that.

At this point I believe it is important to let you know that I believe in being obedient to God, not as a matter of earning one's Salvation, or even as a matter of keeping it, but out of a sense of gratitude for the Salvation, and out of an honest desire to improve the safety of my life. And even this is a bit more complicated than one would see at first glance.

One thing in which many people would find agreement is the idea that the body is a temple, and it should be preserved in good working order. Does that mean that I am a health freak? May it never be! I really can't stand granola products and most "low-fat" stuff is terribly bland to me. But that is just me. I am not saying that is the way things should be for you. Quite the contrary! But, most people who are totally into their bodies are TOTALLY into their bodies, and rarely do anything about their spiritual selves? They don't often do any real thinking on any real deep concerns. But before someone gets their nose out of joint, please realize that this is not a slam on the Fellowship of Christian Athletes[21], or the Power Team[22], or any similar or related group, it is simply a purposeful, and overtly generalized observation. But let's get back on subject, eh?

So, now we have to ask what may be the most important question that can be asked in this profound discussion, and that question is, "What does Kosher mean to you?"

What does Kosher mean to me? Kosher is keeping the whole Law of God, to the best of my ability, as an act of obedience, in appreciation for the Salvation which my Master has given me. Jesus said, "If you love me, keep my sayings." The part about that which always stirs me up is the idea that someone can say they believe that Jesus is Divine – the One True Living God – and then in the next breath say that his "sayings" only include those laid down in the Gospels, or what the Apostles say after the Cross and/or Resurrection, as if He has forgotten his eternal identity or any pre-existing deals that may be in play. Not only does that not make any sense, it isn't even a good example of bad logic. What about the Sermon on the Mount, or the Sermon on the Plain? If Jesus actually is the incarnation of God, did He not also give us all the sayings that are the Law of God from Genesis to Deuteronomy? In this thought it really doesn't matter if one is a Trinitarian or a "Jesus Only" thinker, by what should be standard Christian reasoning, the same one that said, "They will know you by your love for one another" (paraphrased John 13:34-35) also said, "*don't eat that pig*" (paraphrased Leviticus 11:7).

Further, Jesus says;

Matthew 5:17-20 "Do not think that I have come to abolish the Law or the Prophets; I have not come to abolish them but to fulfill them. I tell you the truth, until heaven and earth disappear, not the smallest letter, not the least stroke of a pen, will by any means disappear from the Law until everything is accomplished. Anyone who breaks one of the least of these commandments and teaches others to do the same will be called least in the kingdom of heaven, but whoever practices and teaches these commands will be called great in the kingdom of heaven. For I tell you that unless your righteousness surpasses that of the Pharisees and the teachers of the law, you will certainly not enter the kingdom of heaven."

Jesus says something similar to that several times (Matthew 24:35, Luke 16:17), but the Church seems to find more than a few ways to work around just taking Him at His Word than just to listen. If Jesus says that the Law is important and indispensable, what makes anyone think they can easily dismiss it? If we really stop and think about it, it doesn't make any sense that God would work so hard for 1400 years writing the First 37 books, only to dismiss them as mere object lessons. And, unless you accept them as Law, they are little more than proverbs and parables to ponder.

Further, one should ask a couple of questions, "What does it mean to fulfill the Law?" and then, "What Law or Laws did Jesus come to fulfill?" Does He in fact come to fulfill all of the Laws of the Covenant of Moses? Did he come to fulfill the Laws of Skin Diseases and Mildews in Leviticus thirteen and fourteen? Did he come to fulfill the Law of Pustules in Leviticus fifteen? If so, does that mean that no one will ever get boils again? Does it mean that we don't need to clean our dishes, homes, and materials because mold and mildew will not happen? Does it mean that all this stuff will not happen to Saved People? Does it mean that mold and mildew will not matter anymore? Is there anyone or anything to suggest that the Laws of Sexual Purity as defined in Leviticus chapters eighteen and twenty are fulfilled, or are by any means no longer valid? The answer to all of this is "No." No one would dare suggest that since the Cross it is acceptable to have sexual relations with one's mother or sister. Even if, in recent years, homosexuality has been foisted on the American people in myriad movies and TV shows; that doesn't make anyone really believe that it is acceptable. Is there anyone who would say that Jesus made that one okay? Well, yes, there are those who would tell you that homosexuality is acceptable, but that is a perversion of Law and Grace. Jesus doesn't disavow sexual sin as being done away, and neither does Jesus rescind the dietary codes.

There are those who bandy about a particularly strange phrase that should be mentioned here, and that phrase is "the moral law." By this they mean a collection of laws that they or others have selected as having been established as moral, usually in consideration of being applied in what they seem to think is universal acceptance. But these laws are not universally accepted either, they are just adopted by a given culture – usually a modern American or Western European culture – as having universal application in all cultures. They usually involve such matters as sex, honesty, violence, and property. For those who cite "the moral law" they fail to consider the Plains Indians – oops, Native Americans – who until lately did not consider land as something that could be owned by any person or people. They also don't consider any of the central African cultures that have long

75

participated in child sacrifice or cannibalism. They also fail to contemplate the fact that over two thirds of the cultures of the world allow polygyny (multiple wives), and a few even allow polyandry (multiple husbands). And they don't take into account the fact that Islamic women can be raped, then, for lack of witnesses, executed for infidelity in the matter.

Now is the time to point out that I was raised on pork chops and catfish. Every year, for my birthday, my mother would boil up about a pound of shrimp just for me to eat . . . all alone . . . without having to share. My favorite "date meal" of my youth was surf-n-turf at a good restaurant that made it with fresh lobster and filet mignon, complete with bacon wrapped around the beef. The messages I was given about sex and holiness growing up were pretty much exactly what the World wanted them to be. I had a lot of sexual experience, I smoked, drank a lot, and I fought in tournaments for sport, and in bars for fun, profit, women, and pool tables. I studied and taught martial arts, fought in tournaments, and learned the fundamentals of Zen and the teachings of the East. For a long time I even believed all the evolutionary pseudoscience mumbo jumbo that came with public school. These are the things that I was taught by the culture of my raising.

I tell you this so that you may understand that the things I hold true are not the collective thoughts of my environment. In fact, the paragraph above is the collective thought and belief of my environment. Those are the thoughts that were engrained upon me by my parents, church, schooling, TV, movies, etc. The things that I lay out here are thoughts that come to me by rational, reasonable, and logical examination of the Scriptures, supporting documentation, and the historical record, as a result of my "So What!" moment. And here is a little of what I have learned about this matter.

Martin Luther relied upon what he called "Scripture and Sound Reason." I try to do just that as well, only, unlike Luther, I have Luther and the others to work from as a partial foundation and reflecting pool for my own thoughts.

God alone has the authority to set in order a collection of rules by which we are to live, and has done so. They stand like a fence or a hedge between us and life with the rest of the world. If we stay inside the rules, it is like staying inside the fence of a yard. Inside the fence we are protected from the traffic that is right outside the yard. Does that mean that traffic cannot, from time to time, come crashing through the fence? No, it really does not. But being inside the hedge and fence is obviously different, a vast improvement over standing in the middle of a busy street. Isn't it?

Understanding this analogy, as well as understanding that it is no more flawless than to declare the yard a patently safe place to be; the idea is to maximize the safety and still have a genuinely enjoyable, high quality life. What most people see though, when you mention rules or Law, is the "dos and don'ts." And a part of the "dos and don'ts" lay out like this:

Kosher Eating

76

Is what you eat is to be holy? Does it have to conform to the Law of God in that if it walks or "crawls" on the surface of the earth it has to have split hooves and chew the cud in order to be acceptable (Leviticus 11:2)? If the meat in question is from the waters, must it have had fins and scales (Leviticus 11:9)? If it is a fowl of the air, is it not to be (by nature) a meat eating bird or a carrion bird (Leviticus 11:13-19)? So, to help clarify, the Bible says, pigs have split hooves and do not chew the cud, so they are a "no," and rabbits chew the cud, but have paws instead of hooves, so they are a "no." Not mentioned in the Bible, but easily identifiable, catfish have fins, but no scales . . . "NO." Squid have neither fins nor scales . . . "NO." Hawks and eagles kill to eat . . . "NO." And, what do we do about buzzards? We don't even have to ask. Do we?

For the most part, keeping the dietary part is not that hard unless you get ultra-Orthodox and have to have one stove for meat things and another for dairy things and maybe even a third for Passover. And if you have three stoves, be aware that you also have three separate sets of cookware for the same purposes. But, that all comes from the Talmudic additions to the Law, not from the Law itself.

The hard part of this to accept for many people is that, in this portion of the Law, God sets me free from the bondage of my own, non-beneficial cravings and urges. By making certain things unclean, He puts them out of my reach as foods to be considered, preventing me from having to choose, "Will it be the pork or the perch?"

A Kosher Presentation

Another matter of some concern is that of the shave, the goatee, the beard, etc.

Leviticus 19:27 (KJV)
Ye shall not round the corners of your heads, neither shalt thou mar the corners of thy beard.

Leviticus 19:27 (NIV)
Do not cut the hair at the sides of your head or clip off the edges of your beard.

Leviticus 19:27 (NASB)
You shall not round off the side-growth of your heads nor harm the edges of your beard.

Most Orthodox Jews believe that this means that the beard and sideburns should be left long. Some less orthodox Christians would tell you that this means the beard should be full or not at all. Some of these people would say that a goatee would be an infraction of this law, and that any decoratively cut beards would do the same. But the Scripture passage above regards the practices of the priests of

77

Molekh and others who would actually burn, or brand, or cut, or scrape to scarring, patterns into their beards. So, unless you are planning to purposely harm and permanently scar your face or head, there is likely no sin involved.

Leviticus 19:9ff is full of these sorts of laws we may call the "look different" laws, and the "don't be stupid" laws. In the look different category we find the instruction to be what others may call wasteful in harvesting – leaving the corners and edges un-harvested, and not cleaning up the food left behind after the first gatherer's passing. This made the farms of the Jews an inviting place for travelers to pass by, for widows and orphans, and gave a place for the generally poor to find food. This one is followed by several "don't be stupid" laws that forbid treating anyone unkindly by dealing falsely, oppressing people in any way, belittling them, or even being slow to provide wages. Today, we think of most of these laws as being common sense and caring for one another, but in the cultures surrounding the Jews three thousand years ago, these were novel ideas. And there is much more. Some of them seem rather random, but I suggest reading them, one at a time, pondering them for a while, and seeing how you could apply them to your life. It never hurts to try to improve how we deal with others, and how we relate to God, and how we represent God to the world.

Kosher Marking?

Then there is the matter of tattoos. Yes or no? The truly biblical answer is "no." Leviticus 19:28 (NIV) says, "'Do not cut your bodies for the dead or put tattoo marks on yourselves. I am the LORD." Some read that as do not get tattooed for the dead, but the "cuts" mentioned are for the dead and the tattoos are just tattoos. So, if you are getting tattoos as a form of personal decoration – biblically – that is sin. In fact, the only time someone should be tattooed is if they have no choice in it, such as a slave, child, or wife. In the case of a child or a wife, the husband or chieftain may have the child or wife marked with a tattoo to identify them as members of the tribe, clan, or family. So, it is more reasonable for a woman to have a tattoo given by her husband than for the husband to have one unless he is a slave, or if it is left over from his childhood. Remember that any permanent decoration or alteration of a body is something that should be done by its owner or by the legal steward of that property; and the legal steward doesn't have the right to overrule the owner. Since the owner of all of us is God, and the stewards are either parents, or in the case of a woman, husbands, or masters in the case of slaves, anyone else does not have the right or authority . . . not anyone at all . . . not even one's self.

For those who still contend that the passage addresses getting tattooed for the dead, I would argue that syntax disagrees, but even to them I would mention how many of them have tattoos to remember a fallen friend, family member, or lost child. This is becoming more common every day. If you tune in the Discovery Channel[23] you may come across any of several tattoo shows, and sooner or later you will see someone getting a memorial tattoo. Just a thought.

Next are piercings. There are no explicit passages in the Bible against getting pierced, but it should be noted that the only people that are mentioned with earrings that are not women are the enemies of God. For example, Genesis 35:4 (NIV) "So they gave Jacob all the foreign gods they had and the rings in their ears, and Jacob buried them under the oak at Shechem." Further; Judges 8:24 (NIV) "And he said, 'I do have one request, that each of you give me an earring from your share of the plunder.' (It was the custom of the Ishmaelites to wear gold earrings.)" In both passages the earrings belonged to enemies of the people of God.

Now, women have just about always been, and probably will always be, adorned with jewelry to more pleasingly present themselves to others, especially men. Those men may be the friends of the family, so that the women represent the family well in their appearance, or they may be potential suitors. Sometimes the man for whom the woman is adorned is just her husband. Actually, she should work especially to make herself presentable to him on a daily basis. As to what constitutes an acceptable place to put a piercing, that is extremely debatable.

Today people are finding a whole world of ways to fasten things to their bodies. Historically, jewelry is just hung on loose flesh, such as ear lobes and belly buttons, or the odd nose decoration on the side of a nostril. In a few cultures some women have attached jewels to their foreheads. This is usually done by using glue, like a bindi, or with a pair of skin piercings in the forehead allowing a shaft like that of a safety pin to pass through the upper and lower holes. Sometimes, in more modern settings, the effect is achieved by a pair of brads or even a screw to fasten a jewel setting to the skull. But even that is rather light-weight compared to some of the things people are doing now.

If you look around long enough, in any major city, you will find people that have spikes screwed into their heads and down their backs screwed into their vertebrae. Some of them have rings passing through their wrists or large rings fastened in their backs by which they may be leashed or even suspended. There are lots of people, both male and female, who have pierced their nipples – that is far from uncommon anymore. Less common and far more drastic are men who pierce their penis or women who pierce their vaginal labia. I think in this paragraph, we have crossed the line of what may or may not be acceptable.

But remember, that the pierced people of the Bible have been women, slaves, or enemies of God. So, now it is time to address the second and third categories . . . slaves and enemies of God.

Actually to thoroughly understand this consideration, one must comprehend Paul's position that all people are slaves to something, either slaves of God or something else. Question has always been, and yet remains, "To whom do we belong?" This is a very real question as regards identity. Do we belong to God? If we belong to God, why are we decorating ourselves as if we belong to someone else? For over five thousand years men have worn earrings to show that they were slaves to someone else. For sailors, they were usually marked by having their ears pierced with an awl when they crossed the equator the first time. This was a way of showing that they "belonged" to the sea.

79

In America, in the twenty first century, people would say that they are not slaves, and that slavery is non-existent anymore. However, I would argue that a man with an earring is still a slave, even in America, and even in this century. He is simply not a slave to an individual, but rather a slave to the culture. He has fallen as a victim of slavery to the fads and fashions that are such a profound part of the modern American Zeitgeist. It is all part of the Spirit of the Age that propagates itself by means of Television, Movies, Radio, and News (or what poorly passes for News these days).

Kosher Listening and Doing?

I suggest that any and all of us spend a couple of hours a week listening to some other radio channels than our usual fare. Tune that dial to the station that says it plays the pop music or "hits" – "all hits, all the time" – but not the hits of the past. While there is some of it on the nostalgia channels, the current hits are relentless. What sometimes passes for music these days is absolutely detestable. One singer (not my first choice of term) sings that he wants his girl to put her "ass into it" and she sings back that he should put his "back into it," while a different one sings about her "love humps," regarding her hips and breasts. Still another girl sings about her "goodies" and another guy recalls how he lets his girl lick his "lollypop" and tells her not to stop until it pops, while the girl sings back to him that she wants him to taste her. And in all of these songs there is no mention of marriage, commitment, love, family or even the thought of emotional attachment. It is as though sexuality has become the playground for personal fun without any groundwork and foundation on any level. For the faithful, the body is a temple, but for these people it is an amusement park. Living in Sin? Kosher?

The harder parts are things like the ethical codes that say things like whenever you find something belonging to another person; you are bound by Law to do everything reasonable to return it to the rightful owner. If it is something the owner will actively come seeking, you are to hold it for his arrival – and even provide for its needs if it is a living thing. On the other side of that deal, if you are the owner, you are to pay whatever is reasonable for the care of the lost item, restoring what may have been spent to keep your property in good form. If that item is an animal, you are to compensate the keeper for whatever he may have spent to care for it and feed it, or treat it if it was hurt or sick when it came into your neighbor's care and protection.

Another aspect that is considered passé by the bulk of the Church is the ban on blended fabrics, such as cotton/poly blends. For me and for my application of the Law, all of my shirts are either 100% cotton, wool, nylon, rayon, or something, but not a blend of any. My pants are either all cotton or, in some of my suits they are all silk, or all polyester or rayon. It really isn't that complicated to apply; just read the tags.

When planting crops you may rotate crops, but you don't plant more than one crop in a single field. Now, that doesn't mean that you cannot encircle your veggies with marigolds to keep the aphids away. But it does mean that you are not to plant the crops between one another, as in the same rows . . . like this:

XOXOXOXOX
OXOXOXOXO
XOXOXOXOX
OXOXOXOXO

This was sometimes done when growing in the Fertile Crescent as a way of showing a family's devotion to a particular deity of the area. The modern rationalization of this idea is that two crops may be harvested in different manners that do not destroy one another, and which use up and replenish nutrients in the soil, in a complementary fashion. This practice depends on one plant using what the other is depositing in the soil, and vice versa. The avoidance of the practice is a display that the farmer depends upon the Lord, and not some other deity.

Kosher Sex?

The hardest part for most Americans, most modern anyone really, is the ideas related to sex. People should only have sexual relations with one another when they properly belong to one another, in marriage.

Some years ago, the Evangelical Lutheran Church in America (our denomination at the time) opened a discussion on what was called a (1994) The Church and Human Sexuality: A Lutheran Perspective. In it, the subjects of masturbation and homosexuality were brought up as what may be acceptable sexual behavior and the defecation struck the rotary oscillator with a vengeance. In the discussion there was also a document – a book of the debate theses, essays, and arguments for and against most of the articles of the draft for the Social Statement. Suffice it to say that I had never before seen so many blatantly foolish things being said by otherwise intelligent people with theological degree letters after their names. Some of them were totally dismissing the sexual conduct codes of Leviticus chapters eighteen and twenty as arcane and obsolete. One of them said, "after all, no abstains from sexual intercourse just because their wife is menstruating." But that is a part of keeping Kosher. In a strangely selective division of these laws, they never said that it was okay to have intercourse with their mothers, sisters, or daughters – and none of them advocated sex with animals. And all of these are prohibited in each of these same two chapters.

Remember, sexual activities are only acceptable within marriage. This is not meant to be read as "in a loving committed relationship" either. So, not only is homosexuality a sin, but so is living together without marriage; but I suppose that is why it is called "living in sin."

There are times when to NOT have sex, even within marriage. As mentioned before, one of those times that sex is a "no-no" is during a woman's menstruation. Another is after a child is delivered. Additionally, she may become sexually off-limits as a result of a medical event or condition, such as a surgery or an uncomfortable bladder or yeast infection. Also, she is entitled to sexual pleasure from her husband, as one of her marital benefits, and one of his obligations (Exodus 21:10-11). As for what sexual acts are Kosher: the line appears to lie in the idea that no one is dramatically opposed to what the other has in mind, that no undue pressure is exerted to get there, and that there is no undue damage likely to result from the actions taken, and as long as it doesn't violate some Law of God as regards the act. For example, sex with a non-spouse is out, and for more definite restrictions, one can look at the Leviticus sex chapters (18 & 20). They are quite explicit, though they are not remotely exhaustive.

Again, regarding what is legal for a Judaic-Christian, the only things that explicitly turn up in the Scriptures are male with female intercourse and (poetically) male with female oral sex as mentioned in Song of Solomon 2:3 and 4:16. Also, the idea that just about anything goes is the point of some translations of a Hebrews passage:

Hebrews 13:4 (KJV)

Marriage is honorable in all, and the bed undefiled: but whoremongers and adulterers God will judge.

But the better translation is probably the NIV and NASB versions that seem to warn against behaving in unseemly ways in the marriage bed. The implication within the culture is also that, if one behaved in sexually immoral ways outside the marriage bed, his or her returning to the marriage bed would be to bring defilement there.

Hebrews 13:4 (NIV)
Marriage should be honored by all, and the marriage bed kept pure, for God will judge the adulterer and all the sexually immoral.

Hebrews 13:4 (NASB)
Marriage is to be held in honor among all, and the marriage bed is to be undefiled; for fornicators and adulterers God will judge.

To me, it seems to be saying that the bed that a man shares with a wife is to be kept pure of sexual violations that may put either of them in the position of being an adulterer or fornicator – or as the KJV says, a whoremonger. The King James Version may be read to imply that anything is permissible in the marriage bed. In any event, it is evident that there are other things that can be done or people with whom things can be done that would move a husband and/or wife out of the honor of the marriage bed and into immorality. So, unless we are Missionary Position inclined, we may want to figure out where the boundaries lie, and what those other legitimate options may be. If all a couple is interested in is the Missionary Position, then why define the liberties in the lovemaking. If one doesn't care about what God has in mind . . . well, what's the point in reading this book anyway?

More clearly stated is the idea that kissing and enjoyment of breasts is a welcome activity, as shown in the Song of Songs in this passage:

> Song of Solomon 7:7-9 (NIV)
> Your stature is like that of the palm, and your breasts like clusters of fruit.
> I said, "I will climb the palm tree; I will take hold of its fruit." May your breasts be like the clusters of the vine, the fragrance of your breath like apples,
> And your mouth like the best wine. Beloved may the wine go straight to my lover, flowing gently over lips and teeth.

Kosher Culture & Life!

I really appreciate the struggles of John Winthrop – once governor of the Massachusetts Bay Colony – who felt that in order to make proper laws, crimes should genuinely be identified as sin. But further; sin must be identified as crime and properly punished. His dilemma was, however, to actually and accurately identify what was and what was not Sin. Now, John was a Puritan – not a Baptist or Lutheran – and in his faith, they believed that people should actually study the Word of God and work out their own details. There was no "buying the can" with them. And Winthrop believed that if something was a sin and we said that it was not, the saying so was a sin – and vice versa.

For example: Is it a sin to smoke? If you are a Baptist or a Pentecostal, then the answer that comes to your mind is a resounding "Yes." But, where in the Bible do we find the prohibition on smoking? There is no doubt that it is bad for a person. There is also no doubt that it is an addictive habit and that in itself represents a decided lapse in "self control" which is one of the fruit of the spirit. And if one lacks the Fruit, one may lack the Spirit. And is that a reasonable and logical tautology? Maybe so. Maybe not. I don't know. I quit smoking because I was done being a smoker – not for any deep theological or philosophical reason. It wasn't even because I had fears for my health or life. But then, isn't being a "smoker" a part of one's identity? Well, from a personal point of view, I no longer wanted my identity to be connected to smoking. And if one's identity is in Christ, should it also be in smoke – or any other habit, good or bad? I also believe that someone arranging their resources and opportunities around getting any kind of "fix" is a serious misalignment of priorities.

Now it should be noted that smoking is an exercise of bad stewardship, and it is a bad example to the youth, or weaker brothers, and on those grounds one could make the argument that it is sinful – or at least "sin adjacent" if not sin, in and of itself.

Is it a sin to drink alcohol? Again, some will jump right to "Yes" without a single thought, but we are not here to do anything "without a thought." And again, no regard was given for truth. And keeping Kosher requires right-mindedness about the truth. After all, if one doesn't know what to obey, how can one be truly obedient? The bottom line is that keeping Kosher is more complicated than one may first think, and while some things are not very complicated in themselves, others may well be. Some things are blatant and simple to figure out and obey – a basic dietary code – while others are more complex, like marital law. Some of the codes require digging into the circumstances and the culture of the region at the time of the writing. Some require more social and historical context than others – while some are simple – but all have to be worked out in order to be lived out. That is keeping Kosher.

As for those who try to depose the Law as being only for the people who are "under the Law," and say that when we are under Grace we need not worry about that legal stuff; I would remind them that in Paul's treatises on Salvation in his letters, the concept of slavery plays a huge part. Romans 6:16 tells us: "Do you not know that when you present yourselves to someone as slaves for obedience, you are slaves of the one whom you obey, either of sin resulting in death, or of obedience resulting in righteousness?"

And several times, Paul refers to himself as a slave to Christ. Now, some of the more modern translations may say "servant" or "bond-servant," and sooner or later, some will even say, "employee" or "co-worker," but the word used is that of a slave. It is not even one of higher standing, such as a steward, which would be more specialized indicating some skill, or house steward showing some authority. The word is slave, "δοῦλος," (doulos) meaning a person who is property of another. To exacerbate the idea, Paul continues:

> Romans 6:17-23 (NASB) But thanks be to God that though you were **slaves** of sin, you became obedient from the heart to that form of teaching to which you were committed, and having been freed from sin, you became **slaves** of righteousness. I am speaking in human terms because of the weakness of your flesh. For just as you presented your members as **slaves** to impurity and to lawlessness, resulting in *further* lawlessness, so now present your members as **slaves** to righteousness, resulting in sanctification. For when you were **slaves** of sin, you were free in regard to righteousness. Therefore what benefit were you then deriving from the things of which you are now ashamed? For the outcome of those things is death. But now having been freed from sin and **enslaved** to God, you derive your benefit, resulting in sanctification, and the outcome, eternal life. For the wages of sin is death, but the free gift of God is eternal life in Christ Jesus our Lord.

Following this passage, Paul enters into his dissertation as to how the Law showed him what sin was and therefore, he being aware of sin, was tempted all the more. And this is followed by his dialectic on doing what he should not do and not doing what he should. And in this he concludes, (Romans 7:25 NASB) "Thanks be to God through Jesus Christ our Lord! So then, on the one hand I myself with my mind am serving the law of God, but on the other, with my flesh the law of sin." – so recognizing the duality of his own servitude.

Sanctification – Justification

This shows us the puzzle of Sanctification versus Justification. We are saved and therefore holy, and yet we still have this sin affliction. The process of becoming clean is exactly that, a process. There are those who would tell you that a person gets saved, and if that person is truly saved, they cease to sin. The first problem with that theology is that never actually seems to happen. I have never met anyone that actually did that, and I don't even know anyone else who can honestly say that they know anyone who did it either. The bigger problem though is that if a person, holding this theology, does get saved and then sins, his salvation comes into question and he may never experience a life of Overcoming Christian Faith. Instead, he lives a life of doubt, guilt, and shame. Even if he is actually saved and will live in the house of the Lord forever, he may never truly revel in it or share that joy of Salvation with others in this life.

Does that mean that we should continue to practice sin? After all, where sin increased, grace increased all the more. Paul says, Romans 6:1-2 (NASB) "What shall we say then? Are we to continue in sin so that grace may increase? May it never be! How shall we who died to sin still live in it?"

And one place where Paul would surely agree with John Winthrop is in the discussion of "Who gets to define sin?" Both would agree that sin can only be defined by God, and no other. And since God is not inclined to speak fully and audibly to each of us regarding the definition of each and every possible sin, we need to rely upon His Written Word for that definition, in pointed detail or in principle. But that sounds like legalism, doesn't it? I believe that Jesus and Paul would disagree with branding it as legalism.

Don't forget when Jesus said, "Do not think that I have come to abolish the Law or the Prophets; I have not come to abolish them but to fulfill them." If we recall the complete passage at Matthew 5:17-20, we also recall that Jesus continues this rumination with, "Anyone who breaks one of the least of these commandments and teaches others to do the same will be called least in the kingdom of heaven, but whoever practices and teaches these commands will be called great in the kingdom of heaven." Taking this full text in view, we have to realize that, while failing to keep the Law does not cost one his Salvation, because the one who breaks one of the least of the laws will be the "least in the kingdom," still leaves that person "IN THE KINGDOM." If they had lost their Salvation, they would be outside of the kingdom. Further, "whoever practices and teaches these commands" is promised a greater reward in the coming kingdom.

Now, I have a friend that, when presented with such passages, replies to these ideas with something like, "I resent people trying to get me or anyone else to try to be a better Christian, or tithe more or do more 'works' by using some sort of bribe." And my response is usually something like, "Don't blame me. It was God's idea." God designed each of us to respond to both the carrot and the stick. We each perform better when we know that we are going to receive more benefits of one sort and suffer less pain of another sort. It is in our nature; God put it there, and God uses it, in no uncertain terms. Personally, I would rather do what God has in mind and receive a greater reward than to disobey and get a lesser reward, even if Salvation is not an issue whatsoever. While some may see this as a rather childish point of view, I am inclined to point out that, as with most things in life, these matters don't have to be nearly as complicated as we sometimes work to make them. Sometimes, we just have to hear what is said and do what we are told. Some things are just that simple.

Please understand that in many things keeping Kosher is fairly simple – you do A, B, C, and D – but it is not often very easy. For example, we attended a Lutheran church and we had events about once a month that involve dining with the whole congregation. This usually means a covered dish dinner. Just an aside; I don't say "Pot Luck" because "Luck" is an Eastern Deity of good fortune; a goddess of beneficence. Problem with a covered dish dinner is that of our family keeping a Kosher diet. Of course, we bring things that the family can eat, and we usually make certain to take enough to share plentifully. For example, we took about four dozen all beef hot dogs to one event and most of our family went meatless because the dogs were among the first of things to be consumed. Now, I don't mind bringing six or eight dozen next time, but my irritation is in thoughts like this; "Why would anyone celebrate the birthday of a Jew, whom they readily identify as God, the Law-Giver, with food that the Jew/God has made a law demanding us not to eat?" What is the point of a Christmas Ham? I just don't get it. Why should anyone believe that this is a reasonable idea? I don't, and I cannot help but think that Jesus would frown on it as well.

Sabbath and Rest

Another part of keeping Kosher is the Sabbath. This is the hardest part for me because it seems as though the entire world is against it being done. For starters, most of the Church thinks that the Sabbath is Sunday, but that is a serious misunderstanding of what is going on. The next reason that it is difficult is that so many people want you and me to work on Saturday.

In one sense a man should be expected to do his Honey-do list on Saturday, but as a business owning Computer Genius, I often get called upon to fix computers and solve other problems. My understanding of the Law of Sabbath is that one should do no "servile work," which many rabbis have seen to mean that you should not do what you do for a living. Some have said that this includes any work, regardless of how uncommon it may be for you, other than that which is needful to survive. For example, not only would the mother of the house not cook, because that may be her station of livelihood, but neither can the father, even though he may find it a relaxing hobby.

In an Orthodox household the meals for Sabbath are prepared before and they are of a nature that they will not leave a kitchen mess after eating. So, foods with gravy are out, as are many soups. Most common are sandwiches and vegetables that can be eaten with the fingers and any utensils can be dropped into some clean water without fear of becoming unclean, or better yet, things that can be thrown away. Also common are fruits and vegetables that have been sliced and placed in the fridge in a plastic bag – or if you are too Orthodox for plastic bags, they may be waiting on a platter. Either way, Sabbath meals are usually pretty simple and relatively clean afterward.

The variation to this may be in that some households will prepare the Sabbath meal the day before and it may stay in a crock pot or on the oven for reheating. Just before Sabbath the food may be heated and left on the stove or in the crock, but the oven or crock must be turned off as Sabbath arrives. The cookers may not be working during Sabbath. And I suppose that if one were inclined, one could serve dinner and then wash dishes right before sundown.

Another major place to consider keeping Kosher, is the family unit itself. Paul wrote the Corinthians and said:

> 2 Corinthians 6:14-18 (NASB) Do not be bound together with unbelievers; for what partnership have righteousness and lawlessness, or what fellowship has light with darkness? Or what harmony has Christ with Belial, or what has a believer in common with an unbeliever? Or what agreement has the temple of God with idols? For we are the temple of the living God; just as God said, "I will dwell in them and walk among them; And I will be their God, and they shall be My people. Therefore, come out from their midst and be separate," says the Lord. And do not touch what is unclean; And I will welcome you. And I will be a father to you, And you shall be sons and daughters to Me," Says the Lord Almighty.

This principle of being equally or unequally yoked is most important in marriage, but also useful in matters of business. But in regards to marriage, can you imagine the difficulties that can come from being bound in marriage to a non-believer? Remember that, as a Christian, your father is the God of the Universe, and as a non-believer, the parent is the god of this world; the father of darkness. Talk about having in-law troubles. On one side of the family is the Patriarch, God Almighty, and on the other, Satan, master of all darkness. One can see how family dinners, and more, could be complicated by this kind of family dynamic, but usually, the people involved do not see the spiritual reality that is comically revealed here.

In a business relationship we can see the need to be associated with someone with similar value structures as ourselves. If a business partner places different values on truth, integrity, and loyalty? How may this effect the daily interactions? How will the variance of values effect how each partner deals with customers, vendors, bankers, and more? How may it affect how they handle the books and taxes? You can see how some semblance of agreement is a good thing. How about the relationship of educators to students?

Keeping Kosher is to separate one's self from the World in ways that show the World what is truly expected by the individual that keeps Kosher – as both types of people serve their individual masters in the best way they can. And strangely, it is not intended to be a geographic separation, but a cultural and spiritual one; because you really can't lead anyone to a relationship with the Lord if you are not where they can see you.

Another thought is that of keeping Kosher in the Lord's Supper. But we will address this more fully in an upcoming chapter.

Chapter 6 – The Bible

Regardless of what many people may try to foist on all of mankind, the Bible is the single most reliable and documentable of all ancient documents, and the most important of all documents. It is so significant that most of the other great documents of history find some of their inspiration and philosophy, and often words and sentences, come from the Bible. The Declaration of Independence is a direct mirror of the lesson of Church Discipline presented in Matthew 18.

> Matthew 18:15-19 (NIV) "If your brother sins against you, go and show him his fault, just between the two of you. If he listens to you, you have won your brother over. But if he will not listen, take one or two others along, so that 'every matter may be established by the testimony of two or three witnesses.' If he refuses to listen to them, tell it to the church; and if he refuses to listen even to the church, treat him as you would a pagan or a tax collector. I tell you the truth, whatever you bind on earth will be bound in heaven, and whatever you loose on earth will bed loosed in heaven. Again, I tell you that if two of you on earth agree about anything you ask for, it will be done for you by my Father in heaven."

As you read the Declaration you see the complaint of the people in the British Colonies in the Americas and how they attempted to address them in the smallest terms first, escalated to greater conferencing and finally, taking King George before the global congregation of Christ, they are excommunicating George, and telling the world.

Mechanically speaking the Bible is a collection of what are referred to as sixty-six books, but some of them were divided, such as Samuel, Kings and Chronicles, which had been single texts but had been divided for mass-of-text reasons. If any of those three books were kept in full, they would have been quite cumbersome to carry and read. A couple of books were the compilations of smaller bits, such as Psalms and Proverbs, as well as possibly Ecclesiastes and the Song of Songs. It was given to God's people for the purpose of being the "bread-crumbs" for people to find their way to more clarified understanding of the desires of God in our individual and collective lives.

Probably the best book I have ever seen on the subject of how we got the Bible is called, *From God to Us: How We Got Our Bible*[24] by Norman Geisler and William Nix. In this book they lay out for ordinary people, not theological super-brains, the source of the Scriptures and how they have been transmitted to us. It briefly touches on the prophetic inspiration of the original texts, on textural criticism for "higher" and "lower" criticisms, as well as the collecting of the individual works, the work of the Masoretes, and the creation of the Septuagint. They really do a very good job of making it all understandable by anyone that is actually interested in finding the truth. If, however you are not interested in finding the truth, why bother reading this?

Can You Trust It?

I sat in a class one day and heard someone say something along the lines of, "You can't really trust the Bible, you know. After all, it was first in Hebrew and Greek and then it was translated into Latin as the Vulgate, and then into other versions, and into the King James, then into the current editions that people read. Altogether it has about nineteen iterations before it gets to modern English. So, it's like playing a game of 'Telephone' where one person says something to another, who passes it on to someone who passes it on, who passes it on to someone who passes it on, through a dozen people who each get it just a little bit wrong."

But that point of view is seriously misinformed, and this is not a new position, but is in fact, the prime teaching that allows for Islam to thrive. It has been taught around the world in many ways. But the truth is far more frightening for some people, because it shows the reliability of transmission that has no parallels in the literary world.

The Old Testament was the most carefully transmitted collection of documents of all time. Scribes would work in teams to make certain that a single page would be perfect, letter for letter, line by line, and page by page. If an error was made the scroll would be cut and the new skin would be sewn in to continue the writing and copying. The rabbis that did the work would rather have a document with more sewing on it than a single letter wrong. The content of the Word of God is what was important to them, not its appearance. The scrolls that were made by these temple scribes were always letter perfect, but because it took more people to make less scrolls than anything else, having Scriptures was rare. It was the most carefully transmitted document known to man. There are only dozens of complete copies of the Old Testament, and not even lots of copies of individual books, but the perfection of copying is amazing.

About 900 AD there was a group of Jews called the Masoretes that began collecting bits of the Old Testament so as to assemble a complete and true copy for distribution to all synagogues. Lots of memory and recitation, tons of scraps of parchments, and endless hours of work went into the single, reliable document.

When the Dead Sea Scrolls were found and retrieved in the late 1940's and early 1950's there was among them what is called "The Isaiah Scroll." It is incredibly important because it is a copy of Isaiah in the Hebrew language of the people in centuries just before the birth of Christ. So, some may say, big deal. But this is a big deal because it can be compared directly to the work of the Masoretes and measured, word for word, and letter for letter against their edition of Isaiah, and do you know what is discovered? There is, letter by letter, less than a five percent variance between The Isaiah Scroll and the Isaiah of the Masoretes, and the difference is almost entirely in spelling of proper names and numbers. There are NO doctrinal variations at all from one to the other.

When translating the Bible, no one translates from a translation of a translation of a translation, but we dig into the original words of the ancient texts to translate into modern languages. This is particularly true of the New Testament,

90

of which we have over 5000 manuscripts, some of which are small passages, and some of which are complete letters or gospels. There are even a few complete codices – complete book form texts – that date to within a couple of hundred years of the original writing. By compiling these thousands of documents and comparing them letter by letter, by geography and chronology and more, we are able to trust that the document from which translators work is 99.9% certain to be identical to the original writings by Paul and the guys.

So, instead of having a game of "Telephone" we have an opportunity to translate from exactly what was said by the writers, and to translate these words directly into our language. When one realizes and considers the degree to which our understanding of the original languages has grown, we realize how reliable a translation can be.

Having the understanding that the words can be translated with accuracy is only part of the trust equation; the willingness to accept that the Scriptures are useful to you is another matter. I can only help with a part of that because part of the remaining concern is applicability while more is of historicity. Again, textural criticism comes to the rescue.

When examining the Scriptures you see that they give all appearance of being first-hand transmissions and while someone may say something like, (insert hillbilly accent here) "Well, they could be like that-there book of Mormon, made up after the fact." The literary study of the documents destroy those ideas, because, while a person living now may have the needed studies to assemble a document that looks several hundred years old, because of what we know about ancient documents, a person living "back then" could not. They did not know what we now know about the materials, language structures, syntax, cultural details that would give the document away. With a little time and effort we can now create a document that conforms to the language use of the time of the Revolutionary War. However, this was not true three thousand years ago, or even three hundred years ago. In fact, one of the primary clues to the fraudulent nature of the Book of Mormon is that detailed literary examination shows that it was written entirely by one person, edited by one different editor, and its creation is originated in the first quarter of the nineteenth century, and the location of its origins is within 150 miles of Troy, New York. The point is that a document written in 1200 BC claiming to come from 1500 BC would be spotted as a fraud. The thirty-seven books of the Old Testament were written when they claim to be written, and where. The same is true for the twenty-nine books of the New Testament. If you have more books than that in your testaments I cannot attest their veracity.

Further, when you look at the book and see that it sets its own standard for reliability, which is accurate future prophecy, then the reliability factor increases. In the book of Kings, there is a passage where Ahab, king of Judah, on his way to battle, had a prophet, Micaiah, in prison and set to a diet of bread and water "until I return" to which (1 Kings 22:28 NIV) Micaiah declares, "If you ever return safely, the Lord has not spoken through me." Then he adds, "Mark my words, all you people!" Ahab went to war, dressed not as the king, but in the common garb of a soldier and a random arrow struck him "between the sections of his armor" and killed him by evening. Jeremiah prophesied that Israel would be enslaved in Babylon for seventy years (Jeremiah 29:10 NIV) "This is what the Lord says: 'When seventy years are completed for Babylon, I will come to you and fulfill my gracious promise to bring you back to this place,'" and it was so. Daniel predicted the date on which Jesus would make his "Triumphant Entry" to Jerusalem, and hit the mark to the day. There are over four hundred "types" and prophecies of Jesus that were fulfilled or attributed to Him in His human lifetime. Some of them, like the conspiracies, beating, and betrayal, were completely out of His direct human sphere of influence, meaning that someone else had to do something for them to happen. I would call that reliable.

From a strictly mathematical position, realize that guessing something in the future that either will or will not happen is a fifty-fifty proposition. This means that you have a fifty percent chance of getting it right. If you add another variable then you reduce the odds of your prediction to twenty-five percent. Another variable reduces the odds to twelve and a half percent, etc, etc, etc. But if you have over a hundred variables the odds are drastically against you, and at four hundred variables the odds of all of it happening as expected are astronomical. When you throw in such variables as dates and times, and it has become incalculable.

A pastor by the name of Voddie Baucham[25] responding to the question for his relying upon the Scriptures answers thusly:

> "Why do I choose to believe the Bible? Because it is a reliable collection of historical documents, written by eyewitnesses, during the lifetimes of other eyewitnesses, recording supernatural events, which occur in fulfillment of specific prophetic messages, by men who claim their writings were of Divine rather than human in origin."
>
> "It is written in three languages, on three continents, over a period of 1500 years, with internal corroboration and external confirmation by outside histories and over 23,000 archeological digs, all in agreement, without contradiction."

Poetic Imagery and Not

There are places in the Bible where the language is being poetic or delivering imagery so that you get an idea of something else. In Ezekiel 37 is the passage of the Valley of Dry Bones where God shows Ezekiel a vision of the soul of Israel.

> Ezekiel 37:12-14 (NIV) "Therefore prophesy and say to them: 'This is what the Sovereign Lord says: O my people, I am going to open your graves and bring you up from them; I will bring you back to the land of Israel. Then you, my people, will know that I am the Lord, when I open your graves and bring you up from them. I will put my Spirit in you and you will live, and I will settle you in your own land. Then you will know that I the Lord have spoken, and I have done it, declares the Lord.'"

In this case, God probably doesn't mean that he will be literally bringing the dead to life and returning them to Israel, but that those who are dried up and dead in their souls will be renewed and restored to their homes. After this there will be no reasonable doubt that God had been the power behind the plan, and the voice behind Ezekiel. Unless this is a reference to Matthew 27:52, then this is poetic imagery. In the book of Revelation – recommended only for mature reading – there are passages that describe the New Jerusalem and it says that the shape of the place is a cube that is 12,000 stadia in length, height and width. Realize that a stadion (singular for stadia) is about 600 feet, so that's nearly 1400 Miles in length, height and width – give or take. It says that the twelve gates are carved from single pearls and the roads are covered with precious jewels. God is not trying to give us a blueprint of the place, but an idea that we can carry with us as a mental picture. Keep in mind that the New Jerusalem is actually the Bride of Christ – the Church – and God is conveying to us that it is MASSIVE. It is so large that it cannot be seen, edge to edge from any single place. The doorways are bought with an amazing price and that reflects the importance of the inhabitants. It shows that we are so valuable to God that He gives us pavement of jewels and gold. It is not a design plan, but an expression of our vast number and incalculable value to the Creator of the Universe.

Not poetic imagery is when reviewing history or looking at law and realizing that God actually does not want us to disrespect our parents, and that when Isaac is born, Noah is still alive. Do the math. David did not "figuratively" kill Goliath with a sling and Jesus walking on the water was just that, a walk on the water. I once heard someone say, "Back in those days the expression of walking on the water could also mean taking a stroll on the shoreline." So I asked how it was that Peter became afraid and began to sink. Just a thought! When the Hebrews were escaping the Egyptians across the Red Sea, some scholars claim it meant the Sea of Reeds, so then my question becomes, "How did God get all that water into the lungs of the horses and soldiers to drown them?"

The important thing to do as regards the passages that may be poetic imagery in form is to try to discern what it is that God would have you take away from that passage. Something else that is a form of imagery is the parable.

Parables are stories that may or may not be historical. When considering a parable, the thing that is important is, "What is God trying to tell me in this message?" It may seem like something complicated, and it may turn out to be something very simple. What is important to take away from the parable of the Good Neighbor is not whether it is historical, and it is not that staying at an inn back then was cheap. The message is that the good neighbor is that the Good Neighbor was not me, and then to do something about it. In the parables of the Lost Things we get the overall picture that some things are lost (like sheep) because it is their nature to wander off; some things (like the son) get lost due to rebellion, and some things are lost (like a coin) through no fault of their own, but that when any of these things are found, the parables also tell us that there is great joy and celebration.

Culturalization – When?

In the parable of the Lost Coin we see a woman who has lost one of her ten coins. Some of us look at that and think of dimes, or quarters, but that is far from the facts of the case of the lost coin. What is not explained to us is that having "ten coins" is the common expression for the betrothal crown that is given a bride at her wedding. It commonly has ten coins suspended from a chain or network of chains, that fastens about the brow of the bride. The size, weight and metal of the coins express the value of the bride to the groom. It is his gift to her, much like a ring today. Along with the cash value of the coin there is the sentimental value. The word in the text translated as coin is drachma, which would have been a very well-paid day's wage. In modern terms it may be between 200 and 400 dollars, but it is worth far more to her than even that. It is as if she lost a stone from her engagement ring or wedding set. This more readily explains why she would scour her house and light a lamp to find it. It really is terribly important to her. Another possible element of the parable that may or may not be profound is that the word translated "woman" may also be translated as "widow." Is that what is meant to be heard? It is possible that this is her primary remembrance of her husband. This is just an example of Culturalization that may be needed if we are to fully understand her loss, and her happiness of having found this marvelous thing.

Some Culturalization is going to be less related to the times as much as to the lifestyles. For example, when the law speaks of things that happen on farms and fields, related to livestock or industrial accidents, we can't easily relate. Unless we are out camping or living an Amish life the following passage may never fit into our lives without Culturalization. Take a look.

> Deuteronomy 19:5 (NIV) "For instance, a man may go into the forest with his neighbor to cut wood, and as he swings his ax to fell a tree, the head may fly off and hit his neighbor and kill him. That man may flee to one of these cities and save his life."

A more modern application of that passage may be, "A friend comes over to help you change your transmission and while he is under your car a jack stand breaks so that he is killed, you shall be held guiltless, so long as it is not intentional and occurred without malice." But even that requires some Culturalization because not everyone knows about transmissions and jack stands.

In other passages we need a cultural understanding before we can get an honest grasp of the text. For example, some twenty plus years ago I subcontracted a paper route from a nice young woman who just got tired of getting up that time of day (3 AM). She was in all ways a wonderful Christian woman with one small quirk. She had very long hair, and I commented on it one day and she said that God doesn't want women to cut their hair, and she directed me to a Bible passage:

> 1 Corinthians 11:6 - 7 (NIV) "If a woman does not cover her head, she should have her hair cut off; and if it is a disgrace for a woman to have her hair cut or shaved off, she should cover her head. A man ought not to

cover his head, since he is the image and glory of God; but the woman is the glory of man. Or every man who prays or prophesies with long hair dishonors his head. And every woman who prays or prophesies with no covering of hair on her head dishonors her head—she is just like one of the "shorn women." If a woman has no covering, let her be for now with short hair, but since it is a disgrace for a woman to have her hair shorn or shaved, she should grow it again. A man ought not to have long hair"

For this reason, she had been taught, it was a sin for her to cut her hair and for me to let mine grow long. But what was not done with this verse in her church was Culturalization. It should be explained within the context of the culture into which it was written. In this case, in Corinth, there were many religions that used temple prostitutes and in those temples the women had short hair to give a more "butch" appearance, and the men had long hair to look more effeminate. As for the services of the temples, the women and men working in the temples each usually serviced both male and female customers, er, I mean worshipers, but the men in the city came to these temples in far greater numbers than did the women. The point of the hair styling choices of Paul was to say to the Corinthians, don't look like the whores that serve other gods if you serve the Living God of the Universe.

Another thing to Culturalize is the idea of what is not said, but should be perceived. When Paul writes – or any of the authors – there are collections of understanding that modern Christians do not have, and should if they are to grasp the meaning of a particular passage. This is our failing, not the writers' and not God's. Right after that passage about the hair is a passage about the Lord's Supper. The problem with that passage is that, without Culturalization, everyone thinks it is about a bite of bread and a shot of wine or grape juice. In Paul's day the "Lord's Supper" was an idiom for the Passover feast, it may also be that it is being applied to what has also been termed the "agape feasts" of the days to come. By the time of the death of Cyprian of Carthage in 258 AD the connection between the Eucharist and any substantial meals, such as the Passover, had been terminated. By his time it had been reduced to some form of bread and a shot of wine. But, it is at a Passover feast, lasting up to four hours that Jesus said, "do this in remembrance of me." Because of bad Culturalization, or the lack thereof, the feast has been minimized. It is due to more of the same that the elements have become mystified and deified.

Culturalization as a whole is needed because regardless of how well acquainted we may become with the text, we must remember that the Bible was written to a primary audience; the readers of the days of the writing of each book. If we are to fully understand Paul's writings we must have insights into the cultures into which he writes. Like the haircut thing above, and his Jewish understanding of the Lord's Supper and Baptism, as well as the passage of Romans 7:24 (NIV) "What a wretched man I am! Who will rescue me from this body of death?" In this passage the "body of death" is an idiom from Roman law that expresses a legal sentence. If a man killed another, not through malice, but through negligence, he would be sentenced to a "body of death" which meant that the extremities of the dead guy, the corpse of his accidental killing, would be cut off and the torso would be tied to the negligent killer's back, where it would remain until it was fully putrefied and rotted off the rope. This was the image that Paul is trying to convey when he addressed his failed attempt to avoid sin. He wants us to realize that we are attached to a rotting corpse, and it is our own bodies. Because we applied the Culturalization and find what Paul is actually trying to say, we get the picture that Paul wishes to convey. So, who will save me from this putrefying corpse? "Thanks be to God – through Jesus Christ our Lord!"

Chapter 7 – Law and Grace

To most Christians, the question of Law and Grace is thought of as a question of "Law or Grace," and sometimes even "Law vs. Grace," and that was never the intent. For much of the Church, an idea is commonly held that the Will of God for our lives somehow changed in 30 AD. Many would argue that it happened at the Cross, and some argue that it was in the resurrection, while others may offer Pentecost as the moment of change. But, a serious reality is that this is called Dispensationalism and it really is bad theology.

All too often I have heard from the pulpit the expression, "we would rather err on the side of Grace." But why plan to "err" at all? We all realize that we will make mistakes and that errors will occur, but it seems as though we "plan to err" rather than to "plan for error." But there is a catch, and very few are going to like it. Here's the catch. Ready? The Church, as a whole has been wrong. I don't think that they have, for the most part, lied on purpose; though there has been some of that. It is a simple fact that, by tradition, they have been passed on, and then passed on again, that which was errant. They have in fact erred on the side of Grace.

The initial problem with the "Law OR Grace" approach is that it either concludes with Grace alone and the idea that no one has a behavioral standard at all; or there is the impression leading to making up a "Law" of your own in some sort of pseudo-Christian legalism.

Example: There are church organizations that create rules that they use to define something as Sin. For some this is sex, smoking, drinking, or dancing.

Some promote "sex" as "Original Sin," but that is a pretty serious misunderstanding of that most profound theological term. In some groups, sex for reasons other than reproduction is considered a sin. It is as though even the idea that sex could be enjoyable is a sin to some. But the Word of God is not unclear on these matters (with the possible exception of smoking which is not mentioned at all) but "sin" is not what God calls it all.

As regards drinking, there are prohibitions regarding being a drunk or a drunkard (both are identity terms), but nothing against drinking as a whole. In fact, though Solomon said in Proverbs 20:1 (NIV) "Wine is a mocker and beer a brawler; whoever is led astray by them is not wise." One would be hard pressed to state that this was a statute against drinking. Instead, it is a warning that one becomes foolish when the drink has had its way and the drinker does not maintain his will over it. After all, "whoever is led astray" by anything is not wise, not just drink. Considering dancing, David danced before the congregation of the people of Israel (2 Sam 29:5) "with all his might." In 1 Samuel 18:6 it is shown that dancing was an acceptable form of celebration after David killed Goliath. As David passed through villages, (1 Samuel 21:11) while running from Saul, villagers sang and danced about his exploits.

Sin is a violation of the Will of God. This is primarily defined by the Law of God. There are also times when God reveals a particular plan, and then to violate that specific plan is also sin – even though there is no apparent legal declaration.

In one example, Judah had three sons. The oldest, Er, was married to a lovely woman named Tamar. But Er died. And as was the tradition of the people, Tamar was given to Judah's next older son, Onan, so that he could get her pregnant and have a child "for" Er.

> Genesis 38:8-10 (NIV) Then Judah said to Onan, "Lie with your brother's wife and fulfill your duty to her as a brother-in-law to produce offspring for your brother." But Onan knew that the offspring would not be his; so whenever he lay with his brother's wife, he spilled his semen on the ground to keep from producing offspring for his brother. What he did was wicked in the LORD's sight; so he put him to death also.

In this case, Judah instructed his son, Onan, in the Will of God, and Onan went another direction. So, Onan chose to avoid the Will of God, and – indirectly – Onan chose to die.

Another thing to realize is that the situation above occurred pre-Law. The codified Law would not be handed down from Sinai for 400 years (Deuteronomy 25:5). So, this is not a "Law" matter, in the traditional sense, but is instead a matter of plain simple obedience to the known will of the Master.

It may also be pointed out at this time that, while there is not yet the codified Law of Sinai, there is also some evidence that there was some understanding of Law even before "The Law," and even before the Ark of Noah. Remember that Noah was commanded by God Genesis 7:2 (NASB) "You shall take with you of every clean animal by sevens, a male and his female; and of the animals that are not clean two, a male and his female." And that would indicate that Noah already knew what clean and not clean animals were and how to identify and differentiate them from one another. This fact alone should at least give a clue to the reality of a pre-Law-law.

In another passage

> Genesis 4:3-5 (NASB) So it came about in the course of time that Cain brought an offering to the LORD of the fruit of the ground. Abel, on his part also brought of the firstlings of his flock and of their fat portions. And the LORD had regard for Abel and for his offering; but for Cain and for his offering He had no regard. So Cain became very angry and his countenance fell.

And the reason his countenance fell is that his offering was not acceptable to God as a Sin Offering. It would have passed the later parameters of a grain offering, a fellowship offering, or even a thank offering. But Abel's offering fits the description of a Sin Offering over a thousand years later. But the fact is that there was some sort of law of repentance and an atonement offering, over a thousand years before there was the Big Book of the Law we call Torah.

Again, there is mention of another law before the Law at Genesis 9:6 (NASB) "Whoever sheds man's blood, by man his blood shall be shed, for in the image of God He made man." This "law" is given before common writing (supposedly) and even at a time when there was no community beyond the "Noah" family. But God was preparing them for a time when the situation of Cain vs. Abel would come about again, and He lets them know what is to be done about it.

Would anyone say that Abel and Noah were acting based on Law? Are the actions of these men and their families even some structured part of what we commonly call Covenant? The answer to these questions is, "no." They are all leading and managing their families and leading their worship and practicing their faith in accordance with relationship, instruction, and a personal bond of obedience to the Master of the Universe.

Now, this is a very noble idea, and it really can and does work for people, but the problem is that when people find that their obedience requires a change of direction and giving up something they want, like, or enjoy, they tend to find ways to talk themselves into justifying their desires as acceptable. As for how far this can go, the limits are boundless.

I have witnessed an alleged Christian, a self-professed homosexual saying, on national TV, that there is no contradiction to being a Christian and a practicing homosexual. He said that after doing some word studies into the texts that he said "seem to" prohibit homosexuality, that there was actually no prohibition at all, simply a severe misunderstanding, according to him. Still, the word used in the book of Leviticus to describe God's opinion of homosexuality is *tow`ebah* – הַבֵעוֹת, which appears 117 times in the Hebrew text, and the KJV translates it as "abomination" 113 times, "abominable thing" twice, and "abominable" twice. Regarding *tow`ebah*, Enhanced Strong's Lexicon says, "1 a disgusting thing, abomination, abominable. 1a in ritual sense (of unclean food, idols, mixed marriages). 1b in ethical sense (of wickedness etc)." Other translations use similar phrases, such as a "detestable thing" or "detestation" – but regardless of the translated word chosen, there is really little room for "misunderstanding."

Another modern discussion of what is to be in the "Right" and the "Wrong" columns is that of consuming alcoholic beverages, i.e. beer, wine, hard liquors and even "near beer" and diluted wines. For most Jews, wine is a "given" for most all of life's events, ceremonies, and even religious holidays. For wine to be so important in the primary culture and people of God, then in another to be a sin is either foolish on the part of a people, or on the part of God. Jesus' first miracle was to convert water into wine. But, those who claim that it was fruit juice fail to hear out the passage in which the wine steward says, "Everyone brings out the choice wine first and then the cheaper wine after the guests have had too much to drink; but you have saved the best till now." The implication is obviously that His wine was wine. Besides, "unfermented wine" was not invented until Dr. Thomas Bramwell Welch managed it in 1869, but even his local parishioners did not see fit to do away with the ages old tradition of wine. His son, Charles E. Welch produced it as "Welch's Grape Juice" at the World's Columbian Exposition of 1893. Until that time, all grape juice was either fresh squeezed or fermented, and the fresh squeezed was an extreme luxury, not to be had by many at all. Additionally, the fresh squeezed version would still go bad in a very short time and become a rather disgusting grape-flavored vinegar. In another situation Jesus re-insinuates the alcoholic value of wine in Matt 11:18-20;

> "For John came neither eating nor drinking, and they say, 'He has a demon!' The Son of Man came eating and drinking, and they say, 'Behold, a gluttonous man and a drunkard, a friend of tax collectors and sinners!' Yet wisdom is vindicated by her deeds."

If there had been no wine involved it would have been easy for Jesus to quell the "drunkard" rumors by allowing people to sniff his cup from time to time. But there was no need, since drinking wine would not become a sin for over a thousand years.

As for dancing, well, contrary to what George Strait may sing (*I Just Want to Dance with You*[26]), dancing was invented as a form of worship to the Creator of the universe. Now, we're not talking about the hip shaking, grinding, and gyrating understanding of dance with which so many young and old are familiar. We are also not talking about the Waltz, the Charleston, or the Swing dancing and Jitterbug that followed. No, the invention of dance more greatly resembles praise and prayer dances of Native Americans, Aboriginals of Australia, and many African tribes. These dance forms are not intended to be sexual in nature at all.

Don't get me wrong, most of these peoples have mating, or mate finding dances - and that is the rudiment of most modern dance. It is as though the praise forms of dancing are almost extinct in our more "civilized" cultures. Strange how praise ritual dancing has faded and sexually enticing, and even explicit dance, founded in mating rituals has leapt to the forefront, doesn't sound very "civilized" to me.

When the subject of Sin gets directed at Sex, I would be among the first to defend the virtues of Sex. The reality is that sex is not evil in itself, but neither is money, property, or power. And like the others, it is good or evil in its use. If one is sexually involved with a spouse, and that involvement does not interfere with the rest of life, or damage other relationships, then it is wonderful. If a husband and wife are actually enjoying each other, it doesn't matter whether they are always quiet and slow about it, or if they are wild, loud, and freaky – it's all good. There will be more on this subject in another book. The problems come when the sex they seek is outside the marriage, or if it gets to where the rest of life is impaired by what may be a sexual addiction.

Addiction: this is a word at which we haven't looked. It is an ever present cultural reality, especially in America's own cash-grabbing, gratification driven, entitlement built, self-indulgent, me-ist culture. Wake up call . . . a lot of this is going to come down to addiction, and addiction is going to be attached to identity. As Christians, we are called to be identified with Jesus, not our own actions or even habits. If we are truly attached to Messiah, as we should be, then one of the

"Fruits of the Spirit" is Self-Control. Now this is a subject about which every Christian should be interested.

In the same passage where we find the phrase "fruit of the Spirit" we find the phrase "deeds of the flesh" . . . Why?

> Galatians 5:19-24 (NASB) Now the deeds of the flesh are evident, which are: immorality, impurity, sensuality, idolatry, sorcery, enmities, strife, jealousy, outbursts of anger, disputes, dissensions, factions, envying, drunkenness, carousing, and things like these, of which I forewarn you, just as I have forewarned you, that those who practice such things will not inherit the kingdom of God. But the fruit of the Spirit is love, joy, peace, patience, kindness, goodness, faithfulness, gentleness, self-control; against such things there is no law. Now those who belong to Christ Jesus have crucified the flesh with its passions and desires.

It is my contention that the "deeds of the flesh" are things that are "evident" because they can be seen as moments in time, whereas, the "fruit of the Spirit" should be something that is evident throughout a lifetime. Now here is the catch. The fruit is something that should grow naturally, and it should be a developing result, however, it is also relative to a starting point that is different for each and every one of us. If a person is saved who was a pretty friendly, amiable and compassionate person then he will likely be the kind of person that everyone would love to have for a grandfather. But that is not where most of us begin our journey in the Lord. I know that this description was not me, back in the day. I started out as a hostile, angry, self-absorbed, and lascivious young man who thought nothing of a fight, a hang-over, or thinking that another person was there for little more than my own personal sport. As a result of my jumping off point, I may never be as kind and loving and gracious as someone's unsaved grand-dad, but, I am also nowhere near as mean as I would have been if Jesus left me on my own course. This is where things are about to get really difficult.

If, as the Scriptures say, the quality of our natures called "Self Control" is a natural result, a fruit of living in the Spirit, then why do we so often relinquish that control to other things, such as our own desires and addictions, habits and traditions, instead of striving to discover what God wants of us and using that self control to work out that path? The reasons are various, and for some, the answer may actually be that they are not saved. For others, it is that their traditions have been so ingrained in their core personal values that no amount of discussion, reason, logic, and common sense will ever dissuade them from their disobedience. By traditions, I mean whatever has been drilled into a person by their culture, whether that culture is religious or non-religious or even anti-religious. I have seen disobedience infecting the souls of believers by their own Christian religions in the form of "I don't care what the Bible says; we're having ham for Christmas." And I have heard alleged believers say, "I say grace whenever I am about to enjoy sex with a woman," even though he knows as a single man he should not be having sex with that woman. I wonder, how does he word that prayer? "Thank you Lord for this slutty young woman that I am about to defile, and the prurient pleasures

101

we are about to share." Sounds rather like Pope John XII, who had sex with his niece, raped his sisters, invoked pagan gods, and re-established a brothel in the Vatican.

For some people it is that their own addictions or habits have been approved as non-issues by their organizations or cultures, and, as such, the person addicted, or "in the habit," never makes the personal choice to bring that affliction under the umbrella (so to speak) of Self Control. Sometimes this comes from their educational culture, such as the influences of evolution teaching, Old-Earth theory, presence of extra-terrestrials, sexual liberty, etc. It may be a denominational thing. For most congregations of Lutherans, Methodists, Episcopals, Presbyterians and Anglicans, smoking and drinking are both a non-issue. It can be almost anything that has an ongoing influence in one's thinking and decision making processes and beliefs. And, as we can quickly see, these traditions, culture, education, etc. can lead one down virtually any "primrose path" that one can imagine, and probably some that you or I cannot imagine, and therein lay the need for some sort of control mechanism. This "control mechanism" needs to be something to which all parties can refer as a guide book, or standard. We call that mechanism the Scriptures. And just a side note, when that passage in Galatians 5 said "sorceries" and other translations say "witchcraft" the Greek word used there is φαρμακεία (pharmakeia), which you may recognize as being related to the word pharmacy, and drugs.

I know this from my own experience; I quit smoking because I was tired of being a smoker and wanted to make a change in my identity. I also did not want to be a bad example to others either younger or younger in the Faith. To me, that meant better obedience and conformity. I tried using the patches for a month, but could not afford to continue, so I just became a pain in the butt to my family and friends.

Another point in favor of maintaining the Law to the best of your ability is found in the words of Jesus, from the Sermon on the Mount, and other places where he made a similar point. When Jesus is speaking at the Sermon on the Mount, He is in a virtual huddle with the close disciples on top of the hill, away from the crowds, and he says to them,

> Matthew 5:17-20 (NASB) "Do not think that I came to abolish the Law or the Prophets; I did not come to abolish but to fulfill. For truly I say to you, until heaven and earth pass away, not the smallest letter or stroke shall pass from the Law until all is accomplished. Whoever then annuls one of the least of these commandments, and teaches others *to do* the same, shall be called least in the kingdom of heaven; but whoever keeps and teaches *them,* he shall be called great in the kingdom of heaven. For I say to you that unless your righteousness surpasses *that* of the scribes and Pharisees, you will not enter the kingdom of heaven."

The first thing that should JUMP off the page is that Jesus is not here to abolish the Law or the Prophets. In fact, he says that he came to fulfill the Law, and we will get to that in just a moment. Following forward from that he says that until Heaven and Earth pass away there is to be no change in the Law – at all – not even in the smallest strokes. What does this mean? More importantly, what does Jesus mean by it? And, can we actually know what he means? The answer is an emphatic and resounding, "Yes!" In fact, he tells us right there. He says, "Whoever then annuls one of the least of these commandments, and teaches others to do the same, shall be called least in the kingdom of heaven"

Now, we know that no one can actually annul the Law of God but God, and He is not inclined to do so, but we can treat it as if it were annulled – we can disavow it, and we can teach others to do the same. We can teach that our Grace is sufficient to totally devalue the meaning and value and power of the Law – and even God's right to expect better behaviour from us. To re-emphasize the point, Jesus says, "Whoever keeps and teaches them, he shall be called great in the kingdom of heaven." Wait a minute! Is Jesus telling people that they should "Keep and Teach" the Law of God? Yes, actually, He is. Further, He seems to be implying that there is a graded reward system in place for those who are more or less obedient. After all, those who "annul" the Law will be called least in the Kingdom and those who "keep and teach" the Law will be called great in the Kingdom.

Then is raised the question of, "What did Jesus fulfill of the Law?" For some people, the easiest thing to do is to apply the blanket answer of "everything," but that is not a fair, nor wise assessment of the situation. In fact, the liturgy of most liturgical denominations declares that God sent His Son as a "Sacrifice for Sin and a Model of the Godly Life," and there is the answer. Jesus comes to fulfill the Law of Atonement for Sin of the Penitent. And that is exactly what He does. He did not rid us of our responsibility to be good neighbors or parents, as defined in the Law. He also did not take away our need to make sacrifices for Fellowship or Thanks, or to make restitution for errors or offenses against friends and neighbors and civil authority.

Don't get me wrong; Atonement is a very important thing – especially if you want to enter the Kingdom of God, because none of us can make it on our own merit. This is said to us time and time again, in various ways by different people throughout time. Remember Isaiah 64:6? "All of us have become like one who is unclean, and all our righteous acts are like filthy rags; we all shrivel up like a leaf." Paul would say (Romans 3:23), "All have sinned and fallen short of the glory of God." And (Romans 6:23) the "Wages of Sin is Death." So, obviously, we cannot depend on our own righteousness to get us into the Kingdom, and none of us deserve to get in on our own merit, so we MUST be saved. We must be rescued. That being done, how do we know how we are to behave with our friends and family and the world in general? Well, we cannot depend on our own motivations and understanding to set the standard, can we? "The heart is deceitful above all things and beyond cure. Who can understand it?" (Jeremiah 17:9 NIV) "There is a way which seems right to a man, But its end is the way of death." (Proverbs 14:12 NASB) Nope! We need something that doesn't change with the "whether" – whether we want this or whether we want that.

There should be some consideration given where it says, "until everything is accomplished" we have to remember that part of the "everything"

103

was the devastation of the Earth as in Isaiah 24. If the Earth has not been devastated yet, then "everything" has not passed. Has the attack of Gog occurred and been returned by the "fiery wrath" of God, and did all the "fish of the sea, the birds of the air, the beasts of the field, every creature that moves along the ground, and all the people on the face of the earth [will] tremble at [God's] presence?" (Ezekiel 38:20) The carrot and the stick are revealed above in the statement, "Anyone who breaks one of the least of these commandments and teaches others to do the same will be called least in the kingdom of heaven, but whoever practices and teaches these commands will be called great in the kingdom of heaven." Notice that the disobedient do not get thrown out of the Kingdom, but become least, while the obedient get called "great in the Kingdom."

Beyond this error, many people forget or miss that the Law appears in the Gospel. Many people say that the only laws from the Old Testament that matter anymore are the ones that are re-ratified in the New Testament. There is a long-standing school of thought that says, basically, that the Old Testament is Their Testament, not ours. It is a variation on "that was then, this is now." Some people even say that the Old Covenant or the Old Testament passed away after the cross. But the Old Testament is what Paul and Peter, James, and John used to preach the Gospel. Are we now going to say that they did it wrong?

Even if we are to accept that premise, false as it is, one cannot get out of much. Just think of all of the Old Testament laws that are, in fact, re-ratified in the New. If we are honest in our consideration, the list is very long. Bear in mind, the laws of Atonement are completed with the Death and Resurrection of Jesus, so that takes care of all those laws regarding payment for sin of any kind.

All of the sexual codes remain in full effect because of what Paul and others are thinking as they tell us to abstain from "sexual immorality." We dare not assume that they mean anything other than what God had in mind based on what He already told them, and God told us all what He had in mind, back in the Torah. There are laws that regard finding of things that do not belong to you, but those laws are, more than anything else, good common sense and being a good neighbor. And it seems as though there is a law about washing almost everything, which remains a good idea today. And there is much more.

> Romans 3:27-31 (NIV) Where, then, is boasting? It is excluded. On what principle? On that of observing the law? No, but on that of faith. For we maintain that a man is justified by faith apart from observing the law. Is God the God of Jews only? Is he not the God of Gentiles too? Yes, of Gentiles too, since there is only one God, who will justify the circumcised by faith and the uncircumcised through that same faith. Do we, then, nullify the law by this faith? Not at all! Rather, we uphold the law.

This passage is seen by many as saying that because we are saved by Faith, that Salvation by Faith alone upholds the Law, but that is not what is being said here. The subject of the paragraph is boasting, or more specifically, the lack thereof in our Salvation. Boasting is done away with because Salvation comes by Faith, to both the Jews and the Gentiles, and the rational thought concludes with

"Do we, then, nullify the law by this faith? Not at all! Rather, we uphold the law." The Law is not done away, but rather we are enabled to cope with it, and in accepting the payment of Jesus for all of our sin, the primary need for the Law is Fulfilled, as stated in the Sermon on the Mount. Paul addressed earlier in the same passage that righteousness comes from God has been revealed. It comes "through faith in Jesus Christ to all who believe." We are "justified" by grace through redemption. But that doesn't negate the expected behavior code, does it? No, not any more than becoming a member of a club or family means that you don't have a code of conduct of some sort. Being adopted doesn't mean that you can behave like a baboon on speed during mating season on the Serengeti.

> Romans 3:21-24 (NIV) But now a righteousness from God, apart from law, has been made known, to which the Law and the Prophets testify. This righteousness from God comes through faith in Jesus Christ to all who believe. There is no difference, for all have sinned and fall short of the glory of God, and are justified freely by his grace through the redemption that came by Christ Jesus.

We reflect on our Salvation and realize that it is paid for by Jesus, but we are not free to behave any way that we darned well please, are we? What about Paul saying in Romans 6:1-2 (NIV) "What shall we say, then? Shall we go on sinning so that grace may increase? By no means! We died to sin; how can we live in it any longer?" But if we are going to be dead to sin, does that mean that temptations don't come to us anymore, and if the answer to that is "no" then, how do we decide to which temptations we yield and from which we flee? A man may be tempted by the desires of his wife, but are those desires sin? A man can be tempted in exactly the same way by a neighbor lady, not his wife, and are those desires sin? Most of us would agree that a desire for a wife is not a bad thing in a husband, but a desire for the neighbor lady is a sin. But where did we get that idea? First, we get it from the Law, then from the Sermon on the Mount, where Jesus said it was adultery to look on a woman with lust, much less to act upon it, and then we are reminded of it when the Council of Jerusalem in Acts 15 said a convert to the Faith should abstain from sexual immorality. And we don't really need to define "sexual immorality" any more than Paul and others needed to define it. It has always been accepted as any sexual behavior that involved parties other than husband and wife to one another. And where do we get that? Law, then Jesus, then the rest of the New Testament.

Free From Law

We have all heard it said that we are free from Law because we are saved by Grace, through Faith, and to a determinable degree, this is true. Once we are saved by faith our sins cannot bring judgment of Hell upon us anymore. We cannot be condemned by our actions and lose our Salvation. But one would wonder if we had Salvation in the first place if we live like sinners. By that I do not mean that a slip or a stumble or a failing is good cause to doubt one's Salvation, but a recurring pattern or personality trait may be telling somehow. It may be just that it reveals an area of life about which you need more prayer. It may also be something more severe.

> Romans 8:5-8 (NIV) Those who live according to the sinful nature have their minds set on what that nature desires; but those who live in accordance with the Spirit have their minds set on what the Spirit desires. The mind of sinful man is death, but the mind controlled by the Spirit is life and peace; the sinful mind is hostile to God. It does not submit to God's law, nor can it do so. Those controlled by the sinful nature cannot please God.

Notice some of the key phrases in this paragraph. When Paul says, "those who live in accordance with the Spirit have their minds set on what the Spirit desires" he contrasts between the worldly mind "set on what that nature desires" and the mind of those living in the Spirit. In that contrast he shows the life controlled by "chaim" and "shalom" – life and peace. These are the eternal blessings from the days of Aaron, back when God said, "I lay before you life and death . . . choose life." (Deuteronomy 30:19)

Conversely, "the sinful mind is hostile to God. It does not submit to God's law, nor can it do so." This is particularly telling in that instead of peace, as above, we see hostility. And in our sinful nature we lack the discernment to "choose life" and so we find ourselves, if we are not living in the Spirit, not submitting to God's law, and unable to do so. In choosing the life in the Spirit of Life and Peace we choose to submit because without submission, we "cannot please God." And, don't all of us want to please God? Maybe not! But all of that agrees with the words of the evangelist:

> 1 John 2:3-6 (NIV) We know that we have come to know him if we obey his commands. The man who says, "I know him," but does not do what he commands is a liar, and the truth is not in him. But if anyone obeys his word, God's love is truly made complete in him. This is how we know we are in him: Whoever claims to live in him must walk as Jesus did.

That is some heavy expectation, expecting that we walk as Jesus did. After all, Jesus never did sin and was willing to die for others, even those He neither knew, nor would His friends have liked at all. He made it a point to uphold the Law of God, well above the traditions of men, even those traditions of men ABOUT the Law of God. Jesus looked past whatever people had to say about the Scriptures and read the Scriptures as God meant them to be read. And when the Devil tried to misuse the Word of God, Jesus straightened him out with the Word of God, properly re-applied. And that is exactly what God wants each of us to do as well. That is why He gave us the whole Bible instead of just part of it. That is why He showed us Jesus, Paul, John, Peter, and the rest using the older Scriptures and citing them instead of only using and referring to what some people may call the New and Improved Testament.

> Romans 2:12-16 (NIV) All who sin apart from the law will also perish apart from the law, and all who sin under the law will be judged by the law. For it is not those who hear the law who are righteous in God's sight, but it is those who obey the law who will be declared righteous. (Indeed, when Gentiles, who do not have the law, do by nature things required by the law, they are a law for themselves, even though they do not have the law, since they show that the requirements of the law are written on their hearts, their consciences also bearing witness, and their thoughts now accusing, now even defending them.) This will take place on the day when God will judge men's secrets through Jesus Christ, as my gospel declares.

There is, apparently some degree to which we are found guilty, even though we have had our sins paid for by Christ, because, as Paul says above, "it is those who obey the law who will be declared righteous." Paul, having given his Gospel before, and knowing that it has leaked out, concludes this passage with a statement about this being a matter for the later, more eternal judgment, not a matter for courts or councils, because he says, "This will take place on the day when God will judge men's secrets through Jesus Christ, as my gospel declares." Paul was in Thessalonica only a brief period of time, but the people there had questions about the deeper understandings of the end times. So, Paul may have addressed a certain amount of "end times" theology in his Gospel message as a whole. But the idea of a graduated reward is nothing new.

In the parable of the "talents" Jesus tells of graduated rewards for various levels of performance on the investments made by the stewards. In addressing the lives of the saints built on the foundation of gold laid in the Messiah, Paul says:

> 1 Corinthians 3:12-15 (NIV) If any man builds on this foundation using gold, silver, costly stones, wood, hay or straw, his work will be shown for what it is, because the Day will bring it to light. It will be revealed with fire, and the fire will test the quality of each man's work. If what he has built survives, he will receive his reward. If it is burned up, he will suffer loss; he himself will be saved, but only as one escaping through the flames.

If we look at all the works of our lives and view them as having a positive or negative value, such as "gold, silver, costly stones, wood, hay or straw" and then we plan to take all the works of our lives and pass them through the fire mentioned, then the "wood, hay, and straw" will be burnt up and gone, but the "gold, silver, and costly stones" will remain, and each gets his own reward based on what survives the fire. I posit that the "wood, hay, and straw" are the things that we do that do not advance the kingdom, things that serve ourselves and outright sin.

107

Free To Obedience

But it's not all bad news. The good news is FIRST that Salvation is Free, and it does not depend on you and me. It is a Gift of God, by Grace through Faith in the payment made by Christ Jesus. The further good news is that it is God, in person, who gives us the power to overcome sin on an ongoing and daily basis.

One of the first passages that should comfort the believer is,

> Matthew 11:28-30 (NIV) "Come to me, all you who are weary and burdened, and I will give you rest. Take my yoke upon you and learn from me, for I am gentle and humble in heart, and you will find rest for your souls. For my yoke is easy and my burden is light."

In one of the studies I heard on this passage the idea being addressed was that of a young animal being trained to work with an older, stronger animal. In this case the yoke being used is "easy and light" because it is a much smaller collar mounted below and beside the yoke of the animal actually doing the work. But if that is the intended picture or not is of less importance than the fact that twice Jesus refers to it as "my yoke" and not "your yoke," so we see whose yoke it is and whose burden it is to bear. Another thought from the Master is, (John 16:33 NIV) "I have told you these things, so that in me you may have peace. In this world you will have trouble. But take heart! I have overcome the world." He has authority and is the victor, but even that passage is a bit indirect. It applies to His authority and victory, not yours and mine. For our own good fortune we may rely more upon something like, (Romans 8:28 NIV) "And we know that in all things God works for the good of those who love him who have been called according to his purpose." Where it says, "works for the good," you should read that as, "works for the improvement." It is the Greek word (ἀγαθός) "agathos," and it refers to the intrinsic goodness, not the external qualities of wellbeing or comfort. And that one applies to anyone that loves Him and is called. So, that helps a bit. And the next one should bring peace about our relationship and destination.

> Romans 8:35-39 (NIV) Who shall separate us from the love of Christ? Shall trouble or hardship or persecution or famine or nakedness or danger or sword? As it is written:
>
> "For your sake we face death all day long; we are considered as sheep to be slaughtered."
>
> No, in all these things we are more than conquerors through him who loved us. For I am convinced that neither death nor life, neither angels nor demons neither the present nor the future, nor any powers, neither height nor depth, nor anything else in all creation, will be able to separate us from the love of God that is in Christ Jesus our Lord.

But where do we get help with that obedience thing? This is profoundly important if we truly want to be obedient children of God, even knowing that we have not got the strength within ourselves to achieve much of any value. As the old lyric says, "I am weak, but He is strong."

> 1 Corinthians 10:13 (NIV) No temptation has seized you except what is common to man. And God is faithful; he will not let you be tempted beyond what you can bear. But when you are tempted, he will also provide a way out so that you can stand up under it.

Another personal note from Paul comes as (2 Thessalonians 3:3 NASB), "But the Lord is faithful, and He will strengthen and protect you from the evil one." This passage appears to be expressing that you gain power from Him to have greater resistance "from the evil one." It is important to receive this distinction because it is not just that everything works out, or that the temptations are limited to what you can handle, but also that "what you can handle" changes as your strength grows in Grace. As you become a more mature Christian, you become strengthened, and as you are stronger in your resistance, the enemy will bring more against you, and what he brings will be greater each time. But remember that you are not in this alone. Hebrews 2:18 (NIV) says, "Because he himself suffered when he was tempted, he is able to help those who are being tempted." And the help continues, and grows, and builds, if we participate, because God works for our improvement.

> James 4:7-10 (NIV) Submit yourselves, then, to God. Resist the devil, and he will flee from you. Come near to God and he will come near to you. Wash your hands, you sinners, and purify your hearts, you double-minded. Grieve, mourn and wail. Change your laughter to mourning and your joy to gloom. Humble yourselves before the Lord, and he will lift you up.

Notice the first word in that passage is an active verb, "submit" so you are to be doing something, not to gain your Salvation, and not even to keep it, but by the sheer fact that you are living and continue to do so, you are doing something. God wants that "something" to be submissive to Him. Then we get to begin applying that "Fruit of the Spirit" called Self Control. It is called "fruit" because it should grow in us naturally, like apples on an apple tree. So, if you are a Christian then next year you should exhibit more self-control than last year. If you are self-controlled, and if you resist, look at the reward.

> 1 Peter 5:8-11 (NIV) Be self-controlled and alert. Your enemy the devil prowls around like a roaring lion looking for someone to devour. Resist him, standing firm in the faith, because you know that your brothers throughout the world are undergoing the same kind of sufferings. And the God of all grace, who called you to his eternal glory in Christ, after you

have suffered a little while, will himself restore you and make you strong, firm and steadfast. To him be the power forever and ever. Amen.

"Be" – again an active verb, "self-controlled and alert." There are dangers afoot, but if you "resist him and stand firm in the faith" then in the long term, big picture view of things, God will "restore you and make you strong, firm and steadfast." But what is the dipstick that we can use to measure our progress in our, hopefully, growing life in Christ? According to John that dipstick is our own obedience.

Apparently John, the Apostle of Love, promotes obedience. Because, according to him, if we truly Love we will Obey.

2 John 6 (NIV) And this is love: that we walk in obedience to his commands. As you have heard from the beginning, his command is that you walk in love.

And if he Obeys it will improve his Love of God. Based not only in 2 John 6, but also,

1 John 2:3-6 (NIV) We know that we have come to know him if we obey his commands. The man who says, "I know him," but does not do what he commands is a liar, and the truth is not in him. But if anyone obeys his word, God's love is truly made complete in him. This is how we know we are in him: Whoever claims to live in him must walk as Jesus did.

And that part about "walk as Jesus did" is some pretty big shoes to fill. Not only that, but because we are to "walk as Jesus did" we do not get to be selective about the walk and dismiss part of the walk in favor of another part. Also, because we are already talking to those who are saved, or are claiming to be saved, we are not discussing the subject of getting, gaining, or keeping our Salvation. We are just discussing the Obedient Life that most of us avoid like the plague, and most define as almost anything except the way that Jesus would define it. And for the obedient, the reward is the "completion" of God's Love in them.

James 1:22-25 (NIV) Do not merely listen to the word, and so deceive yourselves. Do what it says. Anyone who listens to the word but does not do what it says is like a man who looks at his face in a mirror and, after looking at himself, goes away and immediately forgets what he looks like. But the man who looks intently into the perfect law that gives freedom, and continues to do this, not forgetting what he has heard, but doing it - he will be blessed in what he does.

As James writes these words to the believers he is speaking to common experiences of all people. Have you ever gotten somewhere and discovered some schmutz on your face, food on your tie, or that your hair is uncombed? Sometimes, when someone looks in the mirror and immediately goes on his way, he just glanced to admire himself, forgetting or ignoring the details of what he has seen. If we look into the mirror and see what needs fixing, a tuft of hair out of place, and collar or toga drape out of place, then does something to fix it, this is the guy that is getting it right. He is improving himself based on what he knows he should see. Likewise, the man of God, wanting to be a better man according to God, "looks intently into the perfect law that gives freedom" and makes adjustments in himself by "doing" what he has seen and heard in the Scriptures.

Perversion from the Pulpits

Over the past thousand plus years there have been insurmountable errors and perversions preached from the pulpits. There have been preaching of racism, anti-Semitism, slavery, anti-nationalism, wars against all kinds of people, monasticism, genocide, but in reality none so great as to compete with selective dismissiveness. Because, by being selective and dismissive toward the Scriptures, all of the rest can be made to seem reasonable. If you can dismiss the governance of the Word of God then what controls are there? The only thing worse than selective dismissiveness is the wholesale dismissiveness of ignoring the entire Bible; but that is usually the result of the unforgivable sin, unbelief.

Here's an example. In the Law there is a passage about a pregnant woman who is caught up in the fight of two men and something happens. Take a look.

> Exodus 21:22-25 (NIV) "If men who are fighting hit a pregnant woman and she gives birth prematurely but there is no serious injury, the offender must be fined whatever the woman's husband demands and the court allows. But if there is serious injury, you are to take life for life, eye for eye, tooth for tooth, hand for hand, foot for foot, burn for burn, wound for wound, bruise for bruise."

Notice the condition of the woman is pregnant. The damage/loss measure has always applied to all persons. No rabbi accepts the "eye for an eye" as being intended for recompense only for men. All persons are covered by this practice of payment in kind. In this case, however, the woman is pregnant and the subject of discussion is found in the next clause after the fight; "and she gives birth prematurely." It is actually the person being born that is to be examined for injury. If there is no "serious injury" then the husband makes demands and the court, or judges, or community elders will determine if his demand is fair, too large, or too small. If the birth is early, but by there being no damage or injury, and it just means that the child will require additional care, then the husband may suggest that the men that fought may have to pay for that care. This is what is meant by "no serious injury."

If the child is damaged in some way then the recompense for the child's injuries is to be the same as if they were the injuries to anybody else. If the child is delivered dead then a life will be charged as the price of the offence. If he has an injured eye, foot, hand, or whatever, you know what has to be done. That's right, matching injuries for the offender or offenders.

Still further Psalm 139:13 (NIV) says, "For you created my inmost being; you knit me together in my mother's womb." The original language word used for "knit" refers to a joining of two items into one. Along with that is the "perfect" tense, which means that it is completed and done, at the time of the verb. Also, "me" is a personal identifier that tells us that what was made is the psalmist, that he was completely made, at the time the two items are brought together to be one. This is God's poetic way of saying that the person to be born is a person at conception.

Now, I know that this is not a popular position, even within the Church, but it is the truth. But even at a scientific level of debate there are some truths to be considered and most of the Church doesn't consider these enough. For starters, if we take cells from the one-day-old cluster of life that results from human sexual conception, and put them under a microscope, the scientist will tell you that you have human tissue. It can even be DNA tested to prove who its parents are.

If you are to hold to the Leviticus (17:11) passage to identify the beginning of life, saying that "life is in the blood," then you would have to contend that any child eleven days after conception is a life because that is when it has blood.

If we were to hold to the same standard in determining "life" as we do in determining "death" which is either a heart beat – in less than three weeks – or brain waves, which show up after only forty days. This is at one seventh of the term of the pregnancy, but still, the baby is fairly well developed.

Still, we cannot get the Church, as a whole, en mass, to agree that killing a baby in the womb is still killing a baby. Since Roe v Wade, nearly forty years ago there have been over fifty five million abortions in the United States. I hear people complain that we haven't found a cure to this disease or that, but in that fifty five million people we killed there may have been the doctor to solve that problem. The next Jethro Tull, the engineer of the end of the potato famine in all of Britain was probably thrown out in the trash of some Planned Parenthood facility. The future Jonas Salk for the AIDS problem was probably left in a bin at some "Women's Health" center that specializes in "in-utero infanticide."

One such operation of ghouls was run by a man named George Tiller, whom you may recall was killed while acting as an usher, who was a member in good standing at Reformation Lutheran Church in Wichita, Kansas – a proud member of the Evangelical Lutheran Church in America. His death factory would gladly murder – oops, er, ah, abort – your baby, even if you were in labor, and as long as you had five thousand dollars. After his death, New York Democrat, Louise Slaughter (fitting) presented a resolution to HONOR the slain child killer, on the floor of the US House of Representatives. How are the mighty fallen when we, the Church of the Living God, cannot muster enough integrity to call this heinous factory of fatality what it is, organized and institutionalized Murder of Children.

So, all of a sudden we find ourselves back at the point of looking to the Bible for a standard of behaviour. Then the discussion opens up to what areas of life the Bible should be able to moderate and how. So, we have come full circle. We are encouraged in (Romans 12:2) "Do not conform any longer to the pattern of this world, but be transformed by the renewing of your mind. Then you will be able to test and approve what God's will is – his good, pleasing, and perfect will."

Don't forget God's words to Isaiah, "Come, let us reason together." The reason for this entire treatise is to get people to bypass their "reflex theology" and to THINK about everything, or in the words of Paul the Apostle, "take captive every thought." Paul would rather that we reason together with God as well.

Thomas Jefferson, one of America's Founding Fathers, said in a letter to a nephew, "Fix reason firmly in her seat, and call to her tribunal every fact, every opinion. Question with boldness even the existence of a God; because, if there is one, he must more approve of the homage of reason, than that of blindfolded fear." As my Life of Christ instructor, Brother David Cook would say, "Christ doesn't expect you to put your brain on a shelf when you come to him." Another teacher said that "Jesus doesn't ask for blind faith. He's left plenty of evidence."

God wants you to think about everything He says and does and requires. Some things are pretty simple to reason out as to why we should or should not do. The laws resembling "thou shall not kill or steal" are pretty easy to understand and reason. Others have taken three thousand years to make sense of them. "Do not cook a young goat in its mother's milk." from Exodus 34:26 doesn't make sense until the twentieth century when we learn that the combination of the meat and the milk damage the value of each. The meat loses part of its protein digestibility from the lactic acid and the milks lactic acid and calcium are rendered almost worthless by contamination from the meat. There are other prohibitions that we may never understand, regardless of how smart we think we are or how advanced our science may seem. We could spend our lives trying to justify individual laws to ourselves because we cannot find a reason for something, but the answers may not actually be available, even after another three thousand years. The best idea is to just do what He says. But that is not reasoning. Is it? No, reasoning is this. In attempting to find God's will for us, we reach into the words of Scripture and find what is to be found.

If that sounds vague, it is vague on purpose. When we approach the Scriptures, we find what God has in mind for us by what is in the text, whether Explicit, Implicit or Derived, but never Contrived. That which is Explicit is plain and means exactly what it says, such as "Thou shalt not steal." The passage regarding marrying sisters (Leviticus 18:18) it is "Explicit" that this should not happen. It is implied, or "Implicit," that having multiple wives is not forbidden. While Leviticus 18:23 forbids a woman to present herself to an animal for sex, it is "Derived" that a man is forbidden from animal sex as well. After all, the beginning of the verse says 'don't have sex with an animal' even before it mentions a woman. I met a woman once that said, based on 1 Corinthians 11:14, Jesus could not have had long flowing locks as shown in all the art of the Renaissance, but must have had short hair. This theological consideration is "Contrived," and this is exactly how to NOT do Theology.

I believe that the Bible is God's gift to us to show us the very best ways of managing what else He has given. I also believe that God has a right to tell us how to live as owner and master. After all, he created us and he bought us, which is two of the three means of coming into ownership. The third way is to receive something from someone as a gift. So, the question now arises, "Have you given yourself to Him?" And if the answer to that question was yes, "Does your behaviour declare it?" Just a thought.

Chapter 8 – Baptism

We all know what Baptism is, don't we? Isn't that where we take someone to the front of the church and dunk them in a big bath tub? Or is it when they dribble Holy Water from a special sprinkler on the head of an infant? Or is it where we meet by the river and dunk them fully under? The process varies from culture to culture and sect to sect, and even sometimes from church to church within a sect. But almost all of these concepts involve water – though some may substitute oil.

Actually, most Biblical references to Baptism have little or nothing to do with water. The "Baptism of John" is all about water in the context of repentance, just like the Pharisees,' but besides that, most are pretty much water free.

In the early passages of the Gospels, we find that the Baptism of John is in and of water as a sign of repentance. In Acts 1:5 Jesus says, "John baptized with water, but in a few days you will be baptized with the Holy Spirit." In this, Jesus is looking back to the Water and forward to the Spirit. Also, one thing that may be considered here is how very little (actually nothing) is mentioned of the Apostles ever being baptized with water, except that a couple of them were followers of John first. We assume it, but we do not read it. They were doing baptisms, but not partaking in baptism.

Later in Acts 2:41 we see, "Those who accepted his message were baptized, and about three thousand were added to their number that day." Many assume water, but is this the Baptism that Jesus spoke of the previous week, saying, "In a few days you will be baptized with the Holy Spirit?" The next Baptism account is in and the story of Simon the Sorcerer (Acts 8:9ff). After people believed Philip they were baptized, and even Simon believed and was baptized, and everyone followed Philip around instead of Simon (a famous magician), because they saw signs and wonders from Philip. If Simon was just dunked in water and was trying to fit in, then the Scriptures need never mention that he "believed" and was baptized. Still, some may question what he believed. Sometime later, Peter and John came and placed their hands on people and they received the Spirit and there was manifest some obvious evidence of the receipt of the Spirit. Many believe that the believers in the crowds that received the Spirit began speaking in tongues. This is not stated and need not be assumed, only that there was some observable manifestation, and those who believe that is was tongues are probably right – in my humble opinion. But Simon the Magician's ego reared its evil head and he wanted the power to dispense The Power. Then he would be the biggest show in town once again and he offered the Apostles big bucks for a franchise in this matter. Peter, being the kind and gentle soul he was said, "May your money die with you." And soon he said, "You have no part or share of this ministry." In the Texican language that would be translated as, "You ain't no partner of ours." Still in all, there's no mention of water. Curious!

In Acts 10 and 11 the discussion comes down to "if God has baptized them with the Holy Spirit, can we refuse to baptize them in water?" It is Peter that reminds us that "John baptized with water, but you will be baptized with the Holy Spirit." Interesting, that in the Simon story the Belief and Baptism came before the presentation of the Spirit, and that in the Cornelius story it was Belief, Spirit and then Baptism.

In Acts 16, at the conversion of Lydia it says "When she and the members of her household were baptized, she invited us to her home." But again, the presence of water is assumed upon the text, but far from explicit in its expression.

The Great Commission

The most famous reference to Baptism is probably the one at the close of the Gospel of Matthew: "Go ye therefore, and make disciples of all the nations, baptizing them into the name of the Father and of the Son and of the Holy Spirit:" And I would argue that this passage has nothing whatever to do with water. And then someone will ask, "Why?" So, in a bit, I will explain.

If we take the above to be the Marching Orders of the Church on Earth, we dare not just accept what someone else tells us Jesus meant. My dad was a military officer and I cannot tell you how many times I heard him say something like, "Don't tell me what you think he meant; tell me what he said." We have to work to find out what is really being said in the text . . . what are The Orders?

For starters, the primary verb in the sentence is not "Baptize," and it is not "Go." I cannot begin to tell you how many times I have heard a pastor giving a sermon, and sometimes a very long sermon, on "Go," and how we cannot stay where we are. The "go" here is in the aorist tense, which means that it has a beginning, but not an ending. Linguistically, it means "while you are going." It is reminiscent of the passage at Deuteronomy 6:6-9 (NIV)

> "These commandments that I give you today are to be
> upon your hearts. Impress them on your children. Talk about
> them when you sit at home and when you walk along the road,
> when you lie down and when you get up. Tie them as symbols
> on your hands and bind them on your foreheads. Write them on
> the doorframes of your houses and on your gates."

The idea of the Great Shema – Deut 6 – is that you will do these things as a matter of whatever else you are doing in your day. While you are going and doing . . . go and do this!

The primary verb of the great commission is "Make Disciples" (μαθητεύσατε), and its form or type of sentence is infinitive - which is rather like a command, or directive. When we tell the kids to take out the trash, or the dogs to get out of the house, this is the infinitive. More like the case with the kids is the case of Jesus in this passage. He is giving instruction to his Children, even giving

116

out orders to his troops. If we tear the passage apart as a Jew would have heard it, it takes on a completely different tone and direction than when we read it like Americans. And it is infinitely important that we read it as a First Century Jew, or Christian Jew, because that is exactly to whom Jesus was speaking. One of the most important things to find in Scripture is what it was that the speaker or writer wanted the listener or reader to experience at that time. It was not written to a bunch of Americans in the twenty century future. This is essential to truly understanding.

Jesus says, "Go, and make disciples." The goal is Disciples. And what are we to do with those disciples? We primarily teach them to "obey everything I have commanded you." (NIV) And we talk about that elsewhere too, but for now, suffice it to say that He doesn't just mean "commanded" in the Gospels. A sub-instruction to the making of disciples is to "baptize them in the name of the Father, and the Son, and the Holy Spirit." To properly wrap your head around this, we have to realize that it contains, and is in fact built upon, three colloquialisms, or idioms. The order I want us to inspect them is actually backward, and I choose this order to de-Americanize it, for the impact that a Jew of the day would get from what was being said.

What if a modern American said this to you: "That dude was so up-tight we had to split just to chill." Would you assume that a city-slicker was fastened vertically in a very snug manner which resulted in someone having to divide in mitosis in order to be refrigerated? No! You would assume that the gentleman was tense, ergo, it was incumbent upon us to depart, for a time, in order to regain some semblance of relaxation. This is what happens when idioms are improperly applied. It could be worse. Some may assume that the "dude" had to be split, ergo, someone produced a samurai sword and divided him in two. But back to the idioms at hand.

First: The Last Clause - - - "the Father, the Son and the Holy Spirit"

Matthew is writing several years after the fact and he has heard vast varieties and versions of the story. All he is trying to do is address a reality in terms by which the readers can relate. Matthew has known something about sectarianism. At the time of his writing there were those hyper-Judaics that were focusing entirely upon the "Father" aspect of God. There was also the old time version of the Jesus-only gang, and the mega-Pentecostals whose total point of concentration is the "Holy Ghost," much like today. Some things never change. So, what Matthew is saying is, "everything that is God." He lays aside the argument of which is what and who is who. As Paul would later say it, "For in him dwelleth all the fullness of the Godhead bodily." (ASV Colossians 2:9). He is simply pointing to the "all in all" of God.

Also, remember that Matthew is, above all else, a Jew. In fact, it is Matthew that bridges the Old Covenant and the New Covenant because he is the one that refers back to the Old in almost every chapter. Matthew brings the images of God into focus by identifying Him in all the "persons" or presentations by which God has chosen to reveal Himself. So, Matthew is referring to everything that is God, rather than focus on any single aspect, or any person or sect's opinion. Also, remember, Matthew uses the phrase "Kingdom of Heaven" where others would say, "Kingdom of God" because to an Orthodox Jew it is improper to use the Name or make direct reference to God. In fact, when writing, most Orthodox, and many Conservative Jews will use the convention, "G_d" instead of writing the word "God." So, if Matthew wants you to think of everything that is G_d, he will refer to His total revealed self as "Father, Son and Holy Spirit." And in the meanwhile, if you have trouble rationalizing the "Trinity" or thinking of "God in Three Persons" as we say in the songs, try thinking of Him as allowing us three different presentations of Himself so that we can see him from three different angles. I know that if I am buying or studying something, it helps to see it from multiple of angles.

Second: The Middle Clause - - - "in the name of . . ." We toss this phrase around in church, in prayers and epithets. We bat it around freely in Sonday School and in platitudes, greeting cards, and at table grace. But what it really means is a combination of thought. The first is that of "by the authority of" and "bearing the authority of" the one mentioned. The second part is that of "in or with the power" of the person whose name is invoked.

In the Roman Empire if the Emperor wanted someone to act in his place in a given territory, he could appoint an Imperial Legate, and that person would speak - not FOR the Emperor, but AS the Emperor. So, when the Legate spoke, gave a command, or wrote a decree, it was as if it were said by the mouth or writ by the hand, of the Emperor. This is where the divergence of thought should take place. The question then is whether the one doing the baptizing is the one with the authority of God, or if the authority of God is being imparted to the one being baptized. In a greater explanation of this point of theology I should express that I actually believe that in this case it is not "either/or" – but both. I believe that the person doing the baptizing is equipped with the authority of God, and imparts the authority of God to the one being baptized. But, more on that later.

Third: The Immanently Important Word - - - "Baptize" It really doesn't mean to dunk someone in water and say some holy phrases over them. Its origins are more related to laundry and clothes making than to theology, and it is exactly those roots that are important. It means to saturate, soak, infuse, dye, and stain. It is immanently important to know what first century Christians would think of what they received. Why? Because it was written to them, in their culture, with their vocabulary and it comes to us by multigenerational inheritance.

When looking at literary and classical Greek references to the words "bapto" and "baptizo" we see that it is used most commonly for dying things (about 65% of the time) and then for soaking, as in laundry or bathing (about 10-15% of the time), and then in lesser instances for general cleaning, rinsing, wetting, dunking (as in the rinsing of food, etc.). It would also be unreasonable to expect that people using a language would choose to apply the least common uses of the words they would so commonly use. After all, the idea of baptism appears several times in the Scriptures, and usually expresses the same idea of application.

There is one passage where a more obscure use of a word is more reasonable than others. This takes place in Philippians 2:5-7 where the better translation is that Jesus did not think that his God-ness should be "exploited." The KJV says that he did not consider it "robbery" and the NIV says "did not consider equality with God something to be grasped." But the NRSV has the better translation in saying, "did not regard equality with God as something to be exploited." But a more obscure application in one place does not recommend a more obscure application in all places. If that were the case then the Bible as a whole would be virtually unreadable. No, because the words appear so many times, in similar context, we have to accept and understand it according to the primary application of the word, which is to dye or infuse. The only variance to that would be the times when the context appears explicit or implicit regarding the application of water. This happens only a few times.

We also have to be careful to not apply the presence of water when the text does not, regardless of what we were told to believe by others. Remember, the primary purpose of this writing is to get people to think – not recite what they have been told.

It also doesn't mean sprinkle, dip, or sop. But that is okay, because in this instance, it has nothing to do with water. It has to do with the presence of God. Let's put it together. A better translation into the language of our day would be more aptly stated as:

"Infuse them by the power/with the power/in the power of the everything-ness of God." This is what Matthew was saying to us.

I wasn't sent to Baptize

One of the main reasons that we have to assume that water has no play in that sentence is based on the understanding of Paul, who was talking about water baptism when he said that it was not a priority for him. In fact, Paul writes to the Corinthians:

> I Corinthians 1:13-17 (NIV) Is Christ divided? Was Paul crucified for you? Were you baptized into the name of Paul? I am thankful that I did not baptize any of you except Crispus and Gaius, so no one can say that you were baptized into my name. Yes, I also baptized the household of Stephanas; beyond that, I don't remember if I baptized anyone else.) For Christ did not send me to baptize, but to preach the gospel – not with words of human wisdom, lest the cross of Christ be emptied of its power.

The attention getter is the passage that should be in the Bold type that says "Christ did not send me to baptize." In that passage, Paul was specifically talking about the water baptism and saying that it was not the intent of his mission. But, if the Great Commission is telling us to baptize, and Paul was not sent to baptize (speaking of water), what is the intent of the Great Commission? Well, if the intent is water, then Paul is either mistaking or misstating his call. And, while it may be possible that Paul is wrong, I would be more inclined to think that it is you and I that make the mistakes in such matters and need to reasonably reassess what is really going on here.

Since we really cannot be talking about the baptism of water, we must be talking about matters spiritual. Understand that if we are talking only of earthly baptism by water, then Paul is saying something equally profound, but also totally different than has been read in this passage. If the Great Commission is for the General Church AND water is the subject AND Paul was not sent to baptize then what is the meaning? Does that mean that Paul is somehow above the General Church and does not need to regard the Commission? Does it mean that the Commission was given to the First disciples only, and that later disciples, like Paul and us, do not need to obey? What is the point and importance?

For now though, let's look at the different means of water baptism and what it does mean and doesn't, and a bit of from whence it comes, and why.

Dunking?

It has been a standing tradition of the Church to baptize by immersion. It appears to closely relate to the baptism of the Pharisees, from whom the tradition is passed down . . . at least, much of the time. When the water was deep enough for such things that is the way the Pharisees would baptize a new convert into the faith of the Jews. However, many are the times that the baptism was done on the Temple grounds, and at those times, the baptism was more likely a matter of pouring the water out on the top of the head. On the other hand, diggings in Jerusalem showed a substantial bathing complex near the Temple, where the 3000 converts of Acts 2 could have been baptized in a single day, and they could all have been dunked completely under the waves. More convincing is the continued practice in Judaism of the Mikveh. The Mikveh (or Mikvah) is the (generically) ceremonial cleansing bath. Specifically it is used most commonly for the re-purification of women after birth or menstruation. In the Cult of Islam it has been bastardized into the bath of the Jihadist prior to a self-destructive attack. It is also the Judaic bath of cleaning in preparation for being anointed as a Prophet, Priest or King.

Sprinkling?

Some would argue that the practice of sprinkling is not very old and definitely not the original intent. But, the Pharisees did something similar when the geography warranted it or weather demanded. Also, the "early Christians" did it. In explorations of the catacombs of Rome, there were several baptismal fonts found with inscriptions, many relating to adult baptism, and many relating to child baptism. In the first 200 years of the Church there was as much diversity on this matter as there is today. Whether there were as many arguing about it as today, we cannot say for certain. We cannot say even that the diversity was a matter of disagreement at all for most Christians, but only that there was diversity.

Some indications are that some of the fonts and tubs were not accessible to people who were not already on the inside of the congregation. There are some indications that one would not meet many fellow believers early in the Salvation relationship because the Church was a hunted entity. Some converts would wait several months before being baptized, and that baptism would take place in the secluded world of the Catacombs, deep in some woods – or some other highly private enclave. This was how the congregation protected itself from the possibility of infiltration and extermination at various times when Christianity was illegal and even punishable by death. I can only hazard to guess that hundreds of thousands of Christians in the first three centuries of the faith were baptized with a sprinkle in the Catacombs . . . in a veritable tomb. It is an interesting image. Imagine entering a newness of life in a place that so greatly resembles a public mausoleum.

Baptism as Anointing

Additionally, the sprinkling appears to more greatly follow the Old Covenant image of the anointing of Prophets, Priests, and Kings – as well as the instruments and dwelling places of God. The Tent of Meeting and the Temple were sprinkled – or splattered – with the "sacred anointing oil" or with sacrificial blood for purification, as dwelling places of God. Aren't we to be the Dwelling Places of God? The instruments of the Temple were also anointed; and aren't we to be His instruments? Even the garments of priesthood are anointed – like we are to be the garments of the Holy Spirit. In the book of Judges there is a passage says "and the Spirit of the Lord came upon . . ." which would be better translated as "and the Spirit of the Lord put on Gideon . . ." as in the passages where the Lord moved the person to action. In the passages of Judges 3:10, 6:24, 11:29, 14:6, 15:14.

Baptism as a Declaration

As mentioned above, there was often a delay in being baptized, introduced to a larger congregation, and led to the leadership of the local family of believers. This was because in much of the Roman world, for a long time, it was illegal to be a Christian, and even more illegal to be a proselytizer. In many cases believers would suffer criminal punishment for their faith, similar to that of being a thief of some sort. But if one were preaching the Gospel, there are still times and places when that is enough to get someone a criminal's execution.

Depending upon who was the prosecuting authority, one could be charged with denial of Imperial Deity, cannibalism (eating the body and drinking the blood of Christ), social insurrection (kingship of Jesus), anti-nationalism (being citizens of another kingdom), treason (declaring allegiance to another king or kingdom) and more. And at these times, it was not very common at all to stand up and make a declaration of faith in a public forum. No, the idea of baptism relating to a public declaration is a fairly new one. It is an idea whose time came into being when it could be inconvenient, embarrassing or socially uncomfortable - not when it could be deadly. There may be a day when we are called to die for our faith, but one would hope that the purpose and profit margin would be better than just, "hey, where do we Christians line up to die?" In many Moslem-ruled countries it is deathly illegal to be a proselytizer – and even punishable to be a Christian. In some Muslim countries one can be jailed for BEING a Christian, and killed for trying to convert others to the faith. Mission work is hard there.

Please understand that I greatly affirm anyone wanting to publicize their earnest faith in their Salvation through Jesus, Messiah. I do not believe that baptism is for that kind of publicity. After all, it takes little or no courage to stand in front of any organization and tell them that you are a member. To stand outside of a Nazi or Klan rally wearing a yarmulke, this is courage – as long as you are truly a Jew and you have business there. To simply put yourself at risk in order to attract attention – this is foolishness.

Baptism as Symbolism for Self

Paul refers once to baptism as being buried in Christ to rise again with Him. In this case, it is a symbol to be remembered in the future. In Israel, they would erect markers for events and commemorations such as in:

> 1 Samuel 7:12 (NIV) Then Samuel took a stone and set it up between Mizpah and Shen. He named it Ebenezer, saying, "Thus far has the LORD helped us."

Likewise, a baptism can be a milestone on the landscape of your life. It can be what says to you, "At this point my life was changed – so I marked it." It can be similar to another rite of passage, such as bar mitzvah, or circumcision. But that is a greater discussion than we are about to enter today.

If a manmade event in your life will help you mark and remember the act and will of God moving in your life, then it is a good thing. The water baptism is there to remind us of the fact that God has done the work in our lives to make us into the children of His Salvation. It is immanently important that we recall that it is God who has done the work, and not us, and the Salvation is His, and not ours. However, if the manmade marking becomes the significant event, that is an error. If the road to Salvation requires that we do something then the road is untrue because Salvation comes through Grace by Faith and not of Works. Remember?

Baptism for Efficacy

Some denominations teach that the baptism of infants or adults insures their entry to the Kingdom of God. Some divisions of the Roman Catholic organization preach that the baptism by Holy Water assures entry regardless of the will, heart, and spiritual condition of the person receiving the rite. In Catholic theology, another rite that is attached to the eternal passage is that of "Last Rites" by which a priest anoints the dead or dying and grants them access by virtue of his position between God and men. But this is contrary to Scripture's saying that no one stands between man and God except the God-man, Jesus, Messiah.

But it is not just the Catholics that make this application. This theological faux pas finds vestigial entrails in the Lutheran, Methodist, Episcopal and Presbyterian churches. It raises its head in the infant baptism ritual that they perform that is often referred back to at funerals. In fact, I have heard it brought up at funerals of people who have lived in such a way as to leave much room for doubt as to whether they ever went to church – much less if they ever met God and joined the Eternal Congregation. This is a grave theological error, if for no other reason than it tends to teach that there is something that we can do to enter the Kingdom and not have to rely on the power of Jesus – which is the only true source of power and access. Further, it indicates that there is something that can be done to a child by his parents that forever alters the relationship between the child and the Master of the Universe. We could possibly be imposing ourselves upon the child in such a way as to nullify his even coming to know the Lord – because, what would really be the point? But also, imposing ourselves upon the Lord and removing from Him all will for repentance from the child and need for relationship. Remember . . . faith, not works. Right?

So, must a Christian be water baptized? The answer is, "no." Should he be water baptized? The answer is, "yes." And how should he be baptized? By whatever means are available and/or necessary. What are the current circumstances? Another consideration is that of the initiates "culture." By that I mean, "How was he brought up and where does he come from?"

Culture!

A pastor/chaplain friend of mine led a young man to the Lord one day and later that young man wanted to be baptized. So, my friend asked where he came from and what his background had been. The young man was from a small Carolina town and Pentecostal family. For this young man it was needful to make a trip to the river. The only river nearby was the raging Chattahoochee, and it is the meanest and most dangerous river in the United States. The water was running at full speed and the size of the young man was no small matter. And to complicate matters further, he could not swim, and, it was warm so the water moccasins could be plentiful. The chaplain had a rope tied to a tree at the river bank and then had it tied the other end to the young man. When the man was dunked beneath the water the chaplain released him, the current swept him away, and the rope swung him to a person waiting by the shore to catch him, as two soldiers stood guard with rifles on top of the hoods of a couple of jeeps.

On another occasion, that same chaplain had presented the Gospel to a soldier and many others, but, days later, on the battlefield, the soldier decided that he would accept the Lord and wanted to be baptized. The soldier was seriously wounded and there was no dragging him to a river or a church. The chaplain spit in his own palm and pressed it to the head of the wounded man and said the words he knew to be true, "I baptize you in the name of the Father, and the Son, and the Holy Spirit." The soldier was saved and as near as I can figure, on that day, all the Will of God was fulfilled.

Even at what most Pentecostals regard as Paul's great baptism story, there is no mention of there being any water involved.

> Acts 19:4-7 (NIV) Paul said, "John's baptism was a baptism of repentance. He told the people to believe in the one coming after him, that is, in Jesus." On hearing this, they were baptized into the name of the Lord Jesus. When Paul placed his hands on them, the Holy Spirit came on them, and they spoke in tongues and prophesied. There were about twelve men in all.

There is a laying-on of hands – which may or may not have been wet. But that too goes unmentioned. The lack of water in the telling is telling.

Early in this discourse we took a quick look at Paul's letter to the Corinthians where he discussed baptisms that he did not do and really addresses the issue of schism and sectarianism. In this, baptism can become a dividing knife. We can get so certain that we are right that we fail to worry, or even think that we could be wrong. He dunks, she sprinkles – We say these words, they say those and all of a sudden, we are totally absorbed in what we do that we totally discount what God has already done.

In the greatest of realities, baptism is what God has done, not something that we do at all. We are baptized into Christ by God. We are baptized in water by one another. One is obviously of greater importance. If I baptized you in water, and God baptized you in the Spirit, which do you suppose will take you into the Kingdom? Just as important; if you are baptized with water and that is all, what is your spiritual state?

So, what is baptism? What is meant by "baptize" in the Great Commission? I would argue that the instruction there is to impart God to the world and to teach them to obey Him.

> Matt 28:18-20 (NIV) "All authority in heaven and on earth has been given to me. Therefore go and make disciples of all nations, baptizing them in the name of the Father and of the Son and of the Holy Spirit, and teaching them to obey everything I have commanded you. And surely I am with you always, to the very end of the age."

Sounds like the same old story; God wants to dwell in the company of the faithful. In the Garden there was one rule and He walked with them. In the desert

He was in the midst of the pillars of smoke and fire, and He walked among his people, and in Revelation:

> Revelation 21:3 (NIV) And I heard a loud voice from the throne saying, "Now the dwelling of God is with men, and he will live with them. They will be his people, and God himself will be with them and be their God.

None of this is new, even for a "New Testament Only" kind of people. Didn't they hear Jesus say, "If you love me you will keep my commands?" Doesn't John say,

> 1 John 1:7 (NIV) "We know that we have come to know him if we obey his commands. The man who says, "I know him," but does not do what he commands is a liar, and the truth is not in him. But if anyone obeys his word, God's love is truly made complete in him. This is how we know we are in him: Whoever claims to live in him must walk as Jesus did."

And this, my friends, leads us to the idea of being obedient, keeping His commands, showing His love, showing our faith BY our works, and keeping Kosher. But what does that really mean and how do we apply it? This is the subject of another text.

> Galatians 3:26-29 (NIV) You are all sons of God through faith in Christ Jesus, for all of you who were baptized into Christ have clothed yourselves with Christ. There is neither Jew nor Greek, slave nor free, male nor female, for you are all one in Christ Jesus. If you belong to Christ, then you are Abraham's seed, and heirs according to the promise.

The LORD bless you and keep you; the LORD make his face shine upon you and be gracious to you; the LORD turn his face toward you and give you peace.

Chapter 9 – The Lord's Supper – Communion - Eucharist

The Lord's Supper is the most common name for a ritual of the Christian faith that finds its roots in a Passover Dinner of 30AD. In the years since myriad traditions have been built up about the event, what to do, what to think, and how to observe its practices. Discussions and divisions about the practices and beliefs revolving around this rite date back to early Second Century and somewhere along the way it went from being a practice, to a habit, to a ritual, to becoming a "Sacrament," which means "Holy Thing" or "Holy Act." And somewhere, sometime ago, it went from being something that Holy people do, to something done to make people holy.

In the Roman Catholic traditions there are many "Sacraments," among which are: Baptism, Confirmation, Holy Eucharist, Matrimony, Holy Confession and Penance, Holy Orders, Anointing of the Sick or Extreme Unction and, finally, Last Rites. In the Roman traditions all of these activities are seen as effectual and recognized as a "Means of Grace" by which Salvation is imparted. This is not an entirely new idea, and it is not a "Catholic Only" idea either. It has roots (at least partly) with Augustine, who once said, "The sacraments of the Old Law were abolished because they had been fulfilled (cf. Matthew 5:17), and others have been instituted which are more efficacious, more useful, easier to administer and to receive, fewer in number." And although Augustine may have been a fairly wise man, neither he nor I, nor any person, place, or agency has the Holy Imprimatur of God in this matter, even if some may claim exactly that.

In all matters Theological, I tend to hold dearly to two dictums of Martin Luther, while, at times, disagreeing with him in the applications and results. These dictums are as follows:

1) Sola Scriptura, Sola Fide, Sola Gratia – only Scripture, only Faith, only Grace.
2) Scripture and Sound (Plain) Reason.

As a background thought of all this and any other Sacramental discussions, we want to bear in mind Ephesians 2:8-9 (NASB) "For by grace you have been saved through faith; and that not of yourselves, it is the gift of God; not as a result of works, so that no one may boast."

Now, there are thousands of books with millions of words designed to convolute this fundamental statement that God has saved you. If you are saved, it is because God provided you with the faith to accept the Gift of Christ, having paid your price of Salvation and nothing more. You and I did not even develop our own faith, because that would be the "result of works," and in thinking this to be the case, we may develop pride in the matter, which is unacceptable.

Some years ago my wife and I attended a funeral for a young man who was of the Roman Catholic tradition. During the funeral ceremony the priest said, in no uncertain terms, that we know that the young man was now in Heaven because he had been baptized; and we know was in Heaven because he had been confirmed; and we know because he had first communion; and because he went to confession. At the end of the sermon he asked that we pray that the departed boy be granted entry into Heaven. Well, that was confusing. It was also terribly sad because I knew that there were many people in that room that believed that if you were baptized, or took communion, or whatever, you would be granted passage into Heaven. But that is not what the Bible says. The Bible says, "by grace . . . through faith . . ."

Efficacy

Another prominent passage on the matter: Mark 16:16 (NASB) "He who has believed and has been baptized shall be saved; but he who has disbelieved shall be condemned." Notice that to be condemned all you have to do is "disbelieve." You do not also have to be "un-baptized" in any way. If you disbelieve you have rejected God's only requirement, and he provides the faith needed to fulfill that requirement. Additionally, if you disbelieve, then you were never baptized by God anyway, no matter how many times you may have been dunked or sprinkled. Since it is His Grace to provide you with His Faith, then disbelief is the "work" of yourself. Everyone knows that they have done wrong. The debt is obvious to even the most hardened hearts. The only payment for that debt is death, and the only way to not have to make that payment yourself is if it is paid by someone else; someone worthy of making that payment – someone pure and sinless. Jesus made the payment that is acceptable to God and the only thing remaining is that you believe. You are designed to believe, as a gift, you are provided with the faith to believe. You can "choose" to disbelieve, but even your own believing is all God's doing.

Real Flesh and Blood

As for the contents and effects of the Lord's Supper, that's debatable. Some teach and believe that the bread and wine become the physical blood and body of Jesus. Some use pressed wafers of bread, while others use a pinch from a loaf of common white bread. Still others use broken crackers, or matzo, and I have even seen it done using Pepperidge Farms®[27] Goldfish® or Ritz®[28] crackers.

I understand the doctrine of Transubstantiation; the belief that the elements of the Eucharist are converted into the actual and physical blood and body of Jesus. I realize that it comes from two passages of Scripture. The first is

John 6:35 and following, where Jesus discusses being the "Bread of Life" that "came down from Heaven." In concluding this conversation Jesus said, "This is the bread that came down from Heaven. Your forefathers ate manna and died, but he who feeds on this bread will live forever." The problem with attributing the passage to actual flesh and blood is that it is forbidden by Scripture to do so. Remember Leviticus 3:17? (NIV) "This is a lasting ordinance for the generations to come, wherever you live: You must not eat any fat or any blood." Let's not forget Leviticus 7:26-27 (NIV) "And wherever you live, you must not eat the blood of any bird or animal. If anyone eats blood, that person must be cut off from his people." As for the flesh, there is a strict dietary code that says that of the things on the land that may be eaten, all must have a split hoof and chew the cud, and humans do neither. The only reasonable answer is that the homily is poetic in nature, and figurative instead of literal.

In the desert Israel relied upon the Manna for their existence, as the provision of God that came down from above. Because it was a physical provision, like bread, it provided for the physical needs, and in the end, all things physical die, as did the ancestors of Israel. "But he who feeds on this bread will live forever." If that lesson were a physical reality and if communion is the physical body and blood, then it stands to reason that everyone that takes communion would live forever physically. Or are we to conclude that Israel of the desert died spiritually as well? If we are talking about Israel dying physically, why, conversely, are we talking about Christians not dying spiritually? The only conclusion that comes to mind should be that in the case of Israel we are talking about physical bread and physical death and for the flesh and blood of the Eucharist we are talking in the spiritual or even symbolic; and symbolic is the most likely. And don't we have several other examples where something physical is representative of something heavenly? The Tabernacle, the Laver, Baptism, Marriage and more represent spiritual realities on a physical earth. Why not the Lords' Supper?

In the passages about the event of the Lord's Supper, I recently heard a pastor say, "Jesus and the disciples were having dinner one night, and Jesus took the bread . . ." The problem with this reflection and representation is that it disconnects from, and maybe even denies the Judaism of the moment. Jesus and the guys, probably with family and friends, children and seniors for the celebration of the Passover; one of the most important celebrations of the Jewish calendar, are enjoying the feast.

As anyone reads the Scriptures, one finds that the Lord's Supper is a celebration of Passover. On this matter I have never met a pastor or Bible teacher who would express any disagreement. However, when it comes down to its Eucharist celebration, it is reduced to a very small shot of wine or grape juice and a cracker or pinch of bread or a pressed wafer. It interests me to look at Jesus, reviewing the whole dinner of Passover, saying, "do this in remembrance of me," and then we reduce it to a thirty second event. It is usually a three to four hour meal with the whole family – and at our house with plenty of friends and lots of food and loads of stories and sharing and wine. But, because of a brief mention in Acts 2:42 (NASB) "They were continually devoting themselves to the apostles' teaching and to fellowship, to the breaking of bread and to prayer," and again in Acts 20:7 (NIV) "On the first day of the week we came together to break bread. Paul spoke to the people and, because he intended to leave the next day, kept on talking until midnight," we break bread, instead of doing a full meal – and we also meet on Sunday instead of Saturday, but to some degree that one makes sense. By beginning our week with Sunday Worship, we offer the first fruits of our hands, heart, and attentions to the Lord.

The Passover is a combination of a dinner party and Scripture lesson that takes from three to four hours, involves a lot of food, four ceremonial glasses of wine, a Scripture test, and a game of find the hidden object. As a part of the celebration it opens with prayers, and there will be prayers and blessings as recitations throughout. It includes several special foods that each has a symbolic meaning in the life of all Jews.

It includes the breaking and hiding of the Afikomen (one of life's most beautiful pieces of symbolism) which is a special cloth envelope that has three pockets for three pieces of matzo bread, which represent the Father God, Messiah, and Spirit. The middle piece (Messiah) is removed, broken in two and half of it is hidden away, someplace in the house, for three parts of the meal; the other is placed back in the Afikomen. After three parts of the meal (until the third day) the children are given the task of finding the hidden piece of bread. Whichever child finds the hidden bread gets a prize; just as whoever finds the Broken Messiah gets a prize. The bread of the matzo is without leaven (sin), it is striped, pierced, and broken. So, at the "Last Supper" Jesus said, "This is my body, broken for you." So, the matzo represents something sinless, that is striped (by his stripes we are healed – Isaiah 53:5), that is pierced (Zechariah 12:10) and broken – or halved – as in the divinity separated from the humanity. While the human flesh of Jesus remains in the grave, the divinity retrieves the prisoners from death of the past. And whoever finds the part that was hidden away for three periods of the meal receives a reward.

Likewise, during the meal there are four cups of wine, each with a special significance. The first cup is the cup of Blessing and opens the meal. The second cup is the cup of plagues or suffering – to remember the plagues and suffering of Egypt. The third cup of Passover is the Cup of Redemption, which denotes Israel being redeemed from Egypt. During the meal Jesus makes what many theologians call the "Words of Institution," as recounted in the Gospels.

> Matthew 26:27-28 (NASB) And when He had taken a cup and given thanks, He gave it to them, saying, "Drink from it, all of you; for this is My blood of the covenant, which is poured out for many for forgiveness of sins."

> Mark 14:24 (NASB) And He said to them, "This is My blood of the covenant, which is poured out for many."

Luke 22:20 (NASB) And in the same way He took the cup after they had eaten, saying, "This cup which is poured out for you is the new covenant in My blood."

Since there are numerous statues forbidding the consumption of blood, if Jesus were talking about having the disciples drink blood he would have been advocating sin, which is very un-Jesus-like. Prohibitions of blood go back to Genesis and show up in Acts, for those who gladly separate Gods Word into "theirs" and "ours." Take a look.

Genesis 9:4 (NIV) "But you must not eat meat that has its lifeblood still in it."

Leviticus 7:26-27 (NASB) "You are not to eat any blood, either of bird or animal, in any of your dwellings. Any person who eats any blood, even that person shall be cut off from his people."

Leviticus 17:10 (NIV) "Any Israelite or any alien living among them who eats any blood—I will set my face against that person who eats blood and will cut him off from his people."

Leviticus 19:26 (NIV) "Do not eat any meat with the blood still in it. Do not practice divination or sorcery."

Deuteronomy 12:23 (NIV) "But be sure you do not eat the blood, because the blood is the life, and you must not eat the life with the meat."

Acts 15:19-21 (NIV) "It is my judgment, therefore, that we should not make it difficult for the Gentiles who are turning to God. Instead we should write to them, telling them to abstain from food polluted by idols, from sexual immorality, from the meat of strangled animals and from blood. For Moses has been preached in every city from the earliest times and is read in the synagogues on every Sabbath."

Everyone at that table knew that the bread was made of the same stuff the bread had been made of for hundreds of years, and not human flesh by any means.

The final cup is the Cup of Praise. Imply and infer what you will, but Church Tradition says that Jesus did not serve that cup, saying that He would not drink 'til all was fulfilled.

The modern Christian failures in dealing with these passages spring from three simple errors. First is the minimalizing treatment of the annual feast that takes days to prepare, hours to perform, and involves a bunch of your personal family; reducing it to a momentary rite of a pinch of bread and a small shot of something, in the company of what may be near strangers. Second is in taking a passage that is intended to be poetic imagery and treating it as some sort of neo-prophetic law. Third is the idea that there is anything that you or I can do that has

130

any effect on our Salvation being imparted or impugned is a human one, and not of God.

When Jesus says, "Do this in remembrance of me," He is at a grand family feast that is winding down and telling them all, when you celebrate Passover (the feast) do so, not just to remember that God delivered the Jews from bondage in Egypt, but that Jesus (God-in-flesh) paid the price to deliver all mankind from bondage to sin. When was the last time you did Passover?

Chapter 10 – Homosexuality

This is such a profound problem, both inside and outside of the Church that it really requires its own portion of attention. The congregation is so full of the world that in the matters of homosexuality they cannot read straight, see straight, or be straight – and by straight I do not mean non-gay. I mean to approach the matter as "straight is the way and narrow the path." I mean that the Church has become ashamed, confused, and even dishonest in this regard, as many have about abortion, so much so that giant congregations and conglomerates of congregations have been led astray by the foolish wisdom not from above.

As mentioned in an earlier chapter, for years the Evangelical Lutheran Church in America (ELCA) was my denomination and in the middle 1990's they began wrestling with the matter of a "social statement" on Human Sexuality. When the draft of the social statement came out, many congregations around the country got a copy. The anger and division, noise and activity at the congregational level, on each side of the discussion, and the counter noise from the clerics was amazing and it was like glass in a blender. There were men and women with high toned degrees and professorships defending pre-marital sex, masturbation, homosexuality, and more. While the social statement became far better than the draft presented first. It took a couple of years for things to settle down, and then, out of the clear blue sky, or maybe it was a cold, black night, snuck in from the Pit of Hell, it became a nightmare of non-scriptural nonsense beyond all measure to the many that left. We were among those that chose to depart. In reality though, it was not our choice, but our obligation. In our congregation at the time several families left, while at other churches whole congregations voted to leave the ELCA. These congregations were wise.

The Selling of Sin

During the hay days of the Third Reich, Adolph Hitler depended greatly on a man by the name of Joseph Goebbels, who served as Germany's "Reich Minister for Propaganda and Popular Enlightenment." He once said, "The bigger the lie, the more it will be believed." Further, his claim to fame, and long lasting influence on the world is in his words, "If you tell a lie long and loud enough, people will eventually start to believe it." There is no part of the American Zeitgeist in which this revelation shines so brightly as in the propaganda of the movement to normalize homosexuality in common thought. If you just look at the television and politics you see that this is true. More on this in a minute. How many style and fashion shows or home décor shows, present homosexuals as more capable in these arena? What you may never see is the homosexual as the bad guy, because if his homosexuality. No, in the Arts in America today, the homosexual must never be vilified, and always be validated.

In the news and political world the "gay vote" is treated as a homogenous and ubiquitous force with which to be reckoned. It is treated as a block that moves in unison as if all have the same interests and priorities. But sometimes they don't. Listen to the news, national and world news, and see how many days you go without hearing anything about "gay" something or "lesbian" something else. And now, the program has changed so that the players cannot be known again without adding in the bi-sexual, transsexual, transgendered, transvestites and whatever new terms come down the pike. And they are all expected to get into lock-step with one another as a voting, thinking, marching unit.

Another question is, "Why is the word 'gay' used in reference to homosexual and lesbian persons?"

When did that happen? In the mid-Nineteenth Century "gay" was used to reference prostitutes, as in "she is a gay woman" or "we stopped at a gay house." This application seems to be transforming toward its modern application by the middle of the Twentieth Century. But even the use of gay as regarding prostitution did not have full effect until after World War II, well after the "Gay '90's." And the "Gay '90's" is a euphemism for a sexually charged period of what certain eras would call "whoring" about.

For the most part it is, as are many things today, the application of a word that means the opposite of the situation. It is rather like the "Ministry of Truth" from Orwell's *1984*[29]. If one looks at the historic meaning of the word "gay" the historic definitions applied, even at Dictionary.com are "having or showing a merry, lively mood, bright or showy, given to or abounding in social or other pleasures." You can add to that happy and joyful. The synonyms offered were: gleeful, jovial, glad, joyous, cheerful, sprightly, blithe, airy, light-hearted; vivacious, frolicsome, sportive, hilarious. These are the historical meanings, but at Dictionary.com[30], the primary meanings have become "1. homosexual, and 2. of, indicating, or supporting homosexual interests or issues." But in general, most people that I have encountered, who are homosexual, and especially the activist homosexuals, do not actually appear very merry or happy, joyous, cheerful or sprightly though they can seem to be showy and as any gay rights parade will show, they abound in pleasures.

Another real trigger phrase that should sound a gong in your hearing is, "not that there's anything wrong with that." Whenever you hear someone say those words, it should immediately come to mind that "there is definitely something wrong with that," whatever "that" is. You will hear it every day, from different people, in different ways, somewhere on TV or movies, if you listen closely enough as one character says of another, "he's gay; not that there's anything wrong with that." Or maybe another says, "She's slept with half the men in town; not that there's anything wrong with that. After all, it really is a little town." "He's an assassin; not that that's a bad thing." See how it works to minimize whatever sins or foibles there may be? "He's a Social Justice attorney; not that there's anything wrong with that."

But make no mistake, it is purposeful, it is pointed, and it is constant by design. To validate this, I challenge everyone that has some satellite TV or digital cable to open up the guide on their service and scan the plot-lines of the shows that are available on the guide. If you have a well loaded cable or dish package and scan through the "guide," up and down the channels, you will find that there is likely not a single hour in a week that does not have some sort of program with homosexuality as a primary or secondary theme. It really doesn't matter if it is presenting the gay player as cute, as in "Will and Grace,[31]" or affable, as in "Entourage[32]," or wise and strong, as in "Torchwood[33]," victimized, as in "The Laramie Project[34]," or common place as in "Happy Endings[35]," or even superior in love and devotion, as in "Rent[36]," the barrage is constant. One of my favorite shows used to be "Glee[37]," but sometimes it felt like a ride on a pride parade float, so it is off my list. Some days you may have to reach out thirty minutes or even two hours for people and areas with limited service. Some services can boast five hundred channels, and reviewing the options one sees as many as twelve hundred shows with homosexuals or homosexuality as primary plot device in a single day. Other examples are that virtually every medium makes accommodations for homosexual and lesbian proclivities. Check out AOL, Netflix, Amazon, and more.

Some people like to toss about the phrase "homosexual agenda" as if it is a unified and comprehensive plan with every detail worked out by every homosexual and agreed upon, down to the very last prancing protagonist in the parade. But this is not the case. It is a grand scheme orchestrated, for the most part, by people that really seem to believe that their lifestyle is a valid and honest option, available to many or all. It is enhanced by those who approach the matter as with sympathy for the downtrodden, much like the abolitionists of the nineteenth century. Then it is exacerbated by those who would normalize homosexuality because that is one step closer to finding acceptance for their own proclivities. This is especially true for members of NAMBLA (North American Man/Boy Love Association), which is a haven for pedophiles. But homosexuality is not acceptable for God, and should not be acceptable for His people, but then again, neither is pedophilia.

Culture and Situation

One of the things that kept coming up in discussing many of the subjects of "Social Statement on Human Sexuality" was the argument of "that was then, this is now," and attempting to qualify why one behavior or another would have been untenable in their culture, environment, or situation; but not so much today.

Some professors of Lutheran Seminaries (and others elsewhere) have argued that the reason that homosexual practices were unacceptable was that they had to preserve their population and that their small numbers in the wilderness put them at risk. According to these voices, any sexual activity that could not result in conception would be unproductive, ergo wrong, and that was why they were banned. But that argument fails when we realize that a man who is married to sisters, or bound in marriage to moms and daughters, the relationships could still produce offspring. Also, this is hardly a well reasoned consideration as their numbers have been estimated variously between one and three million. Some scholars guess lower and some higher, but with little foundation for their conclusions. After all, in the beginning of the book of Numbers it says:

> Numbers 1:1-3 (NASB) Then the LORD spoke to Moses in the wilderness of Sinai, in the tent of meeting, on the first of the second month, in the second year after they had come out of the land of Egypt, saying, "Take a census of all the congregation of the sons of Israel, by their families, by their fathers' households, according to the number of names, every male, head by head from twenty years old and upward, whoever *is able to* go out to war in Israel, you and Aaron shall number them by their armies.

The end result is a count of 603,550 of those described in that passage; the age of twenty and above and "whoever go to war in Israel" and at the age of fifty you became eligible for retirement, even from the priesthood. So we are numbering Males only, ages twenty to fifty, which would indicate that (given the life expectancy, etcetera) that means that this group is somewhere between a half and two thirds of the Male population. If we split the difference, that makes the Male population about One Million people. If we consider that there is approximately the same number of Females (statistically females usually number fifty two percent of a stable and monogamous population) then we have a total number of about Two Million. If not for the provision of the Lord by sending manna and quail, this number of people could have starved to death trying to live off the land and wandering in the wilderness. In a non-monogamous, polygynous population, the females may comprise as much as two thirds of the population, and can therefore give birth with much greater frequency. Their problem was not trying to keep their population UP, but down. But, for the most part, the hard life took care of that. In the twenty sixth chapter of Numbers the population is counted again and they come up with a total of men, in the same age range, of 601,730 – within a one half of one percent margin of error of the original number; and this was after a generation of people had died, all except Joshua and Caleb, and of course, Moses, who would be left behind and soon die. So, since these people were more likely to starve than to suffer at the hands of marauders or brigands, and since the same people did meet in conflict with other peoples and win, then we can earnestly assume that their problem with homosexuality was not in maintaining a population minimum, but in the very homosexual actions themselves.

Another thing to point out is that this is not a Situational Ordinance of any kind. It is not put in place to offset a specific condition of the day so that, when that condition no longer existed the law could be rescinded. A Situational Ordinance is a law that is to be fulfilled when a specific circumstance exists. If a people are stranded in a wilderness, they may have to pool all of their resources, until they are rescued. But this is not a call to socialism. If a neighbor has livestock that wonders off and you find it you are to care for it, patch its wounds and feed it as needed until that neighbor comes to get it. When he comes for the animal he is to remit payment for whatever expense and trouble the beast may have been to you. Notice the situations? If the neighbor's cow wanders you care for it . . . if you were to take the animal without it wandering into your possession, this is called larceny. The care and keeping of the animal is conditional upon the animal wandering. Don't forget that the owner of the animal is responsible for the cost of any needs of the animal, as well as any damages it may do. With regards to homosexuality, and all of the sexual codes, God doesn't give any reason to believe that they would be changed when the congregational circumstances change. And really, aren't we still wandering in a desert, making our way to the Promised Land? So, the circumstances remain pretty much the same.

Sodom and Gomorrah

Beginning with Sodom and Gomorrah we see destruction of a pair of cities, and while the story is old and the reasoning obvious, this is where the argument begins, not, however, where it ends. In fact, the average position-defending homosexual claiming Christ would direct you to look at Ezekiel where it says:

> Ezekiel 16:46-50 (NIV) Your older sister was Samaria, who lived to the north of you with her daughters; and your younger sister, who lived to the south of you with her daughters, was Sodom. You not only walked in their ways and copied their detestable practices, but in all your ways you soon became more depraved than they. As surely as I live, declares the Sovereign LORD, your sister Sodom and her daughters never did what you and your daughters have done. "'Now this was the sin of your sister Sodom: She and her daughters were arrogant, overfed and unconcerned; they did not help the poor and needy. They were haughty and did detestable things before me. Therefore I did away with them as you have seen.

And while that person may point out that Sodom was not destroyed for homosexuality, they miss the greater point. The Scripture notes that the people being warned "walked in their ways and copied their detestable practices" but that they "soon became more depraved than they." Can you imagine what it takes to be more depraved than Sodom? The text tells us in no uncertain terms when it says, "Now this was the sin of your sister Sodom: She and her daughters were arrogant, overfed and unconcerned; they did not help the poor and needy. They were haughty and did detestable things before me." Sodom's sin was haughtiness and arrogance. They put themselves above and beyond even the rule and design of God. They got to be so full of themselves that the fundamental rules of life did not seem to apply to them anymore. Even the basic design and functions of the bodies in which they lived did not matter anymore. So, in the one sense, the homosexual priest is correct in that the core of the sin is not the homosexual behavior. The sin is the Arrogance and Haughtiness, whose ultimate symptom was homosexuality. In this way the homosexuality is like the running nose of a cold. The running nose is not the illness, but a symptom of the cold. When the cold is eradicated the runny nose clears as well, and so clears the symptom of homosexuality when the haughtiness and arrogance is replaced with humility and submission. Still, don't forget that it says, "They were haughty and did detestable things before me." They still DID DETESTABLE THINGS. What is it that the men of Sodom and Gomorrah did? Oh, yeah, that would be the demands on the houseguests of Lot, and those pesky homosexual acts.

Chapter 11 – Identity

And that is what Paul tells people has already happened and will happen, when he addresses the Corinthians;

> 1 Corinthians 6:9-11 (NIV) Do you not know that the wicked will not inherit the kingdom of God? Do not be deceived: Neither the sexually immoral nor idolaters nor adulterers nor male prostitutes nor homosexual offenders nor thieves nor the greedy nor drunkards nor slanderers nor swindlers will inherit the kingdom of God. And that is what some of you were. But you were washed, you were sanctified, you were justified in the name of the Lord Jesus Christ and by the Spirit of our God.

> 1 Corinthians 6:9-11 (NASB) Or do you not know that the unrighteous will not inherit the kingdom of God? Do not be deceived; neither fornicators, nor idolaters, nor adulterers, nor effeminate, nor homosexuals, nor thieves, nor the covetous, nor drunkards, nor revilers, nor swindlers, will inherit the kingdom of God. Such were some of you; but you were washed, but you were sanctified, but you were justified in the name of the Lord Jesus Christ and in the Spirit of our God.

The most powerful part of the passage is when Paul says, "And that is what some of you were," or "such were some of you." This is all in the past tense. Their being identified as one who is sexually immoral, idolater, adulterer, effeminate, or homosexual had its conclusion at the "but" of that sentence, which says "but you were washed." The part where it says "you were washed" is three words in English, and only one word in Greek. In Greek the word is "apelousasthe" (ἀπελούσασθε) which is in the aorist tense which can best be expressed as an event that had a point in time where it began, but continues to be into the future. So, a clumsy, but more accurate translation might be "but you have been and continue to be washed." The point of the text is that the washing cleaned away the sinful identity of their earlier life and continues to do so. And isn't identity what it is all about?

"Who is he?" The officer asked a witness. The witness replied, "He is just some guy who . . ." and he continued to give a description. The guy was short or tall, black, white or something else; he wore certain clothes, had a limp or big hair, some kind of hat, and did a certain thing, but none of that is who he is. That is the question of identity. We use words and identifiers to know who we are and who others may be. We use words like Father, Mother, Christian, Jew, soldier, marine, Son, miner, teacher, killer, anchorman, and theologian. These are words that describe what we do as part of our identity and or part of our family or social position. Some describe achievements like doctor or champion, while others describe conditions like prisoner and invalid. And sometimes they describe something profound like belongingness or not, as in the first letter of Paul to Timothy when he says this:

> 1Timothy 1:8-11 (NASB) But we know that the Law is good, if one uses it lawfully, realizing the fact that law is not made for a righteous person, but for those who are lawless and rebellious, for the ungodly and sinners, for the unholy and profane, for those who kill their fathers or mothers, for murderers and immoral men and homosexuals and kidnappers and liars and perjurers, and whatever else is contrary to sound teaching, according to the glorious gospel of the blessed God, with which I have been entrusted.

He starts by talking about "those who are" and he calls them "lawless and rebellious," but then he begins using identifiers instead of modifiers. He doesn't say they did ungodly things and sinned, but calls them ungodly and sinners. That is the difference between the testimony of a witness saying that someone did something, and someone able to tell you who someone is in their identity. These people are "the ungodly and sinners," and they are "the unholy and profane," and "murders" which is clarification of what they do as, killing "their fathers or mothers." Then he hits another list of identifiers that is a subset of the first in the list, "immoral men" (men without morality), and saying that they are "homosexuals and kidnappers and liars and perjurers," which is again, by no means a complete list, because Paul finishes of by saying whoever else "is contrary to sound teaching" is equally guilty. At this point I would like to tie this discussion back to the Sermon on the Mount, and the most difficult passage for most pastors and Christians in general to digest. Why? It flies in the face of their generally lawless upbringing. Check it out. Matthew 5:19 (NASB) "Whoever then annuls one of the least of these commandments, and teaches others to do the same, shall be called least in the kingdom of heaven; but whoever keeps and teaches them, he shall be called great in the kingdom of heaven." The "commandments" about which Jesus speaks is the Law – usually accepted as the laws of Leviticus and Deuteronomy that don't deal directly with atonement.

Sound teaching is what Paul mentions and associates the evils and identities of the evil ones as being connected to "whatever else is contrary to sound teaching," and Jesus says to disciples (people on the inside already) that anyone that breaks (annuls in the NASB) or devalues these commands or teaches others to do the same will lose reward in the Kingdom. And remember that Jesus is talking to His People, not outsiders. These are the guys that will make up his inner circle someday and help save the world. A thought that should come to the mind of the serious reader is that if you don't always share, that is not a sin, but if it is a part of your character so that you could be identified as a "skin-flint" then that may indicate that you are not one of the people on the inside, but on the outside because the Scriptures are full of admonitions to be giving and caring and sharing, even to the strangers that pass by unseen. And remember that Peter says, (2 Peter 1:4 NASB) "For by these He has granted to us His precious and magnificent promises, so that by them you may become partakers of the divine nature, having escaped the corruption that is in the world by lust." Since God is a giver and we "may partake in the divine nature," then giving should be in our nature – after a while – and if it is not, then we would have to wonder if we are in a position to partake of the divine nature after all. If a person claims to be a Christian and is a skin-flint, is he deceiving himself about his faith position, or was he such a selfish and stingy dirt bag when he got saved that being a simple skin-flint is still an improvement that, maybe, those who have known him can see?

And here is the big deal; if you are any of those on one of these lists, you may well not be a Christian, and that should be of no small concern to you. Remember that these lists are not complete. There is not an actual dipstick with which one may check his or her Christianity, but there are some indicators that one can examine from time to time. Start with the "fruit of the spirit" in Galatians 5:22-23 (NASB) "But the fruit of the Spirit is love, joy, peace, patience, kindness, goodness, faithfulness, gentleness, self-control; against such things there is no law." If you have no one you love and if you are miserable and angry and impatient and unkind, if you cheat on your wife and business partners, kick dogs and yell at kids and you smoke, drink, do drugs and can't kick the gum chewing habit, then you are probably not saved at all. But most of us don't begin to fit all those criteria. Do we? Still, we are all guilty of something, and as Paul says, we fall short of the Glory of God. And if you are a homosexual, or a child rapist, or a kidnapper, or a perjurer, then the odds of you being a Born Again Christian are worse than drawing to an inside straight-flush, which is 52 to 1, and that is probably generous. However, if you are one of these people and want to get saved, what are the odds? Better than even money, if you are earnest. And then there is "Don't ask – Don't tell" then again, Proverbs 14:34 (NASB) "Righteousness exalts a nation, But sin is a disgrace to *any* people."

If we, as a people, approve of homosexuality, or any other evil identifier, then we become a reproach (KJV), and history shows how bad an idea that is. The Northern Kingdom of Israel became a reproach and it was gone. The Kingdom of Babylon became a reproach and they were replaced. Assyria became . . . I think you get the point. More recently, how long did it take for Germany and Japan to get over the consequences of their evil works in World War II?

Paul also points out, even in his more condemnatory statements, that there is redemption for those who are far away from God's intent and design. Remember in the Corinthians statement he said, "such were some of you; but you were washed" but more personally, he said of himself, in 1 Timothy 1:13 (NIV) "Even though I was once a blasphemer and a persecutor and a violent man, I was shown mercy because I acted in ignorance and unbelief." In this statement he is not saying that he participated in a gay rights parade, but that he participated in or oversaw the murders of the saints, and yet he was redeemed. Even though he was in a direct conflict with the Creator of the Universe, the Author of the Law and the Puppet Master of the Prophets, he was salvageable, and God salvaged him very well. Before he died, Paul went from being a scourge of the Church to being one of the greatest of evangelists in the history of the Church. So, while you still have life in your limbs, there is hope.

Nature or Nurture

One of the realities is that there have been literally dozens of studies done on the subject of whether homosexuality is genetic, but there are studies to show that every sin or shortcoming is genetic. In the last couple of decades the "genetic" team in the argument finally found a couple of studies that landed on their side. Until then, all other studies said that homosexuality was not a genetic predisposition. One of the other realities in the discussion is that both of the studies that concluded that homosexuality was a genetic predisposition were run by homosexuals whose prior and extant predetermination was that homosexuality was genetic. The primary premise of the "scientific method" is that you approach an experiment with a hypothesis (what you believe is the answer) and then you try to prove it wrong, using every empirical means of validating and invalidating each option and possibility.

The most scientific question about those two outstanding studies that concluded that homosexuality is genetic is: "Were the experiments contaminated by purposely skewed research, data, or analysis of the data?" It's not like there were never any homosexuals involved in any of the previous studies, but in only a couple of studies were the conclusions different, and there may have been less than scientific reasons for it. Given the world of politics and public opinion and gay/lesbian influence in entertainment and education in America, the general goal appears to be that of acceptance and approval, just like at Sodom and Gomorrah.

As mentioned before, the Evangelical Lutheran Church in America decided that it would be a good idea to ordain homosexuals as pastors and ministerial assistants. And to be fair, the ELCA has come down on the wrong side of most of their Social Statements in the past twenty years. They speak for endless reams of rambling and spin, to contort their way onto the wrong side of Abortion, Death Penalty, Economic Life, Education, Environment, Genetics, Health and Healthcare, Peace, Sexuality, Race, Ethnicity, and Culture. They aren't terrible as regards "Peace," but non-committal and weak, and their approach to the Environment is strangely reminiscent of the most liberal, and out-there, California tree-hugging, bird lover. But that is what happens when one tries to run a huge congregation by over-educated and self-inflated egos. But, Don't Take My Word for It, or theirs.

Regarding identity, the most important question available is, "Is your identity in Christ?"

Chapter 12 – Obedience

When will we find ourselves being obedient, without calling obedience a sin? When will we believe that God in Christ knew from day one that He had a plan for us and we didn't? If we can overcome our own desires and let God have control we may find that we have a much simpler life. I don't mean that we will wake up Amish one day, but we can enjoy the simplicity that God has in mind for us, even in our complex world. I once heard someone say that they were glad (at the time) that we had a President like Clinton, instead of Reagan. I replied that, even with the Alzheimer's, I would rather have Reagan because, even with memory problems, Reagan did what he believed to be the Right Thing, and not what would benefit him personally. I wish we could get Ronny back today.

But getting back on track, we have seen in several places in the Bible, especially in Judges, where the people of God began to do what God required and life got better. And then, "The Israelites did evil in the eyes of the Lord; they forgot the Lord their God and served the Baals and the Asherahs." (Judges 3:7 NIV) It's like churchgoers worshipping at the temples of Ford, GE, and Starbucks. This is what Israel did, time and time again. They would be put in their place, follow their charter, then "they forgot," and then "they served" something else.

How many of us serve something else? We don't have to think of it as a "god" in our life, but may see it as a need, a want, a right, or a just reward. Do you have a dozen pairs of shoes, live in a million dollar house, drive a car that is a blatant waste of space, fuel, and money? Is there a friend or neighbor you could help out of need? I don't mean one of those on the news whining that life is unfair and someone needs to take responsibility for their mistakes, bad judgment, and welfare mentality. But maybe there is a neighbor that could use some help fixing his car to get to work, or maybe it is just a bus-pass. Have we made our own desires more important than the needs of our brothers?

How about some simple stuff? Cotton-poly shirts? Bacon with breakfast? Did your last haircut come from a place with a "Book of Mormon" available on the counter. Did you give a Jehovah's Witness some money to go away? Were you part of that church on the East Side that rented out space to a Mosque? Did you have shrimp quesadillas or Jimmy Dean Pork Sausage today? Are you living, or trying to live a godly life, God's way? And if the answer is "yes," are you looking in the Bible to see if you can identify God's way? Or are you looking at what someone "says" is God's way? Or are we as arrogant as someone that believes that God's way is not for us, not needed, not wanted? Are we without the needed humility to say, "Yes, Lord, I will obey?" And it really is a matter of humility, because, without it, we are lawless, self-serving, whore-mongers, gluttons, homosexuals, and effeminate, slothful ne're-do-wells and Sons of Belial. Ecclesiastes 12:13-14 (NIV) The Conclusion of the Matter

Now all has been heard; here is the conclusion of the matter: Fear God and keep his commandments, for this is the whole duty of man. For God will bring every deed into judgment, including every hidden thing, whether it is good or evil.

And this is the crux of the matter, the purpose of the entire book, and in reality the purpose of the Bible as well, to get people to think about what it is that God wants them to believe and what he does for them every day as they live. Remember the words of God, speaking to Cain after the failed offering event, (Gen 4:7) "If you do what is right, will you not be accepted?" God has always wanted us to do the right things. But in order to DO the right things, we must know the right things, and that is why God told us the right things. If we find an excuse to not do the right things, we find ourselves being arrogant, like the people of Sodom, which is not living in the blessing, but in the cursing. So, be humble.

Micah 6:8 (NIV) He has showed you, O man, what is good. And what does the Lord require of you? To act justly and to love mercy and to walk humbly with your God.

Remember the key point of Ezekiel 16:49 (NIV) "Now this was the sin of your sister Sodom: She and her daughters were arrogant, overfed and unconcerned; they did not help the poor and needy." The arrogance led to the life of sin and debauchery, but humility leads to obedience which leads to being concerned, helping the poor and needy, doing what God says to do. So 2 John 6 (NIV) says, "And this is love: that we walk in obedience to his commands. As you have heard from the beginning, his command is that you walk in love."

Are we going to be humble and obedient, doing what God has in mind for each of us as much as possible? Or, are we going to be arrogant and order that bacon cheese burger, put on our cotton-poly wardrobe, let the government tend the poor, and claim to be good Christians?

Common Sense and Christianity

Common Sense and Christianity is thinking about our Faith, plainly, honestly and simply, asking the obvious questions, and seeking the most ordinary possible answers, without yielding to our own presuppositions. It is looking at the Holy Writ and seeing what is there instead of what we have been told is there, or what we want to find there. More than anything we have been told what to believe by our denominations, parents, TV, and everything else we encounter along the way all of our lives. The irritating part of that is how much all of those have been lied to and led to believe misinformation all of their lives. It is not like they are actually trying to fill you with falsehood, only that falsehood is embedded in everything they know.

In the computer programming world there is an expression: GIGO – Garbage In Garbage Out. It is a rather flippant way of saying that if your programming is in error then error is the result. It is just as true in human life as it is in computer programming. Take a look at a couple of thoughts.

143

If you grew up in a socialist country that was without major events of political dissatisfaction you may well believe that government by socialist engineering is normal, even preferable to other forms of government. If your socialist homeland had periodic uprisings, even riots, if you were allowed to know what the riots were about, you would likely grow to suspect that there may be something wrong with socialism. You may begin to explore the histories, practices, and results of alternate forms of governance and may even choose to help bring about change.

A person who grew up in a culture that devalued sexual intimacy to where it was treated as a form of amusement without attachment, pleasure without commitment or consequence is likely to think this is normal. Such a person may even believe that this is the way things are supposed to be; but it is not. You and I know this because we have had some sort of corrective input to our consciousness that informs us of the right and wrong in these matters. But even that input is not thorough and complete, or reliably correct, even if we have been Christian for a long time.

If we have been Born Again there may be new born ideas in our minds that seem to resemble little light bulbs coming on in our heads. As we read the Scriptures these light bulbs become brighter and more numerous and reach farther and farther into our subconscious and conscious thoughts, hopes and desires. They slowly illuminate the recesses of our minds and piece by piece the world makes better sense to us and we understand just a little more. The biggest problems in all of this are that so much of the Church still has so much of the World in it, and sometimes worse, it has so much un-scriptural Church tradition woven into the general theology. And the traditions of men, which Jesus railed against, have persisted for nearly two millennia. Remember, Mark 7:8 (NIV) "You have let go of the commands of God and are holding on to the traditions of men." And some of the "traditions of men" revolve around the definition and understanding of God's Grace and His Salvation for you. So, you can see that it is rather important that we get this stuff right.

Jesus put it quite succinctly when he said, Mark 7:13 (NIV) "Thus you nullify the word of God by your tradition that you have handed down. And you do many things like that." This was the case then, among the Jews, and even more so now. There are, in fact, more "Christian-ish" traditions and activities than there are Christian actualities.

Think about it. How many people wear a cross or crucifix to protect them? How many go to church on Christmas and Easter? How many people each day go to mass or every week to church? How many people genuflect when confronted with an obstacle in their lives? How about Easter Eggs, christenings, catechisms, and a collection of "sacraments" and rituals to rival any secret society? But what is the truth?

144

What is Christianity?

Contrary to the words of some, Christianity is a religion, but it is a religion based in a sound relationship with the Creator of the Universe. In that respect it is like Judaism. In fact it is the logical progression of Judaism before the rational conclusion of all things. Historically there was personal relationship in the Garden, followed by Patriarchy and family altars. Later there was tribalism and Covenant, with Abraham and sons, followed by Law, by the Word of God and the hand of Moses, and enforced by the Prophets and the Writings, which combine to form the foundations of formal Judaism.

From the time of the Garden until the complete fruition of Judaism there were prophecies about the coming Messiah that was born to the world during the reign of Rome in Israel. At sometime about four to six years BC God came, in person, as Jesus; was born in Bethlehem, and He lived a sinless life so that He could be our Sacrifice for Sin and a model of a Godly Life. But that is the history, not the definition. I cannot stress it enough, tell it enough, or feed you the Gospel enough to have done enough; so here we go again.

Christianity at its most primal is the simple culmination of thought that says this:

1. I am a dirt-bag sinner, worthy of death and Hell, and so are you. (Romans 3:23 NIV) "For all have sinned and fall short of the glory of God."
2. All my sin must be paid for, or else I cannot enter the eternal rest of God's home, because it leads me into the Eternal Prison of Hell – the "second death." (Romans 6:23 NIV) "For the wages of sin is death, but the gift of God is eternal life in Christ Jesus our Lord."
3. Jesus paid the price for all my sin by dying on the Cross. (Romans 5:8 NIV) "But God demonstrates his own love for us in this: While we were still sinners, Christ died for us."
4. If I believe that this is true, His payment is credited to my account and I am forgiven and may live forever in His Kingdom, I am saved, and it is also true for you. (Romans 10:9-10 NIV) "That if you confess with your mouth, 'Jesus is Lord,' and believe in your heart that God raised him from the dead, you will be saved. For it is with your heart that you believe and are justified, and it is with your mouth that you confess and are saved."

Once you believe then you are saved and you enter a relationship with the owner of all things, God, who then promises certain things as a part of the relationship; Covenant. The Covenant says that you agree that He has done the work to save you, then you receive the blessings that follow. These are different for each believer, but they will be there all the same. Some have received some of the gifts mentioned in the Bible. There have been some who have received musical genius as a gift, or some other sort of useful skill. The "natural" result or fruit of the relationship includes, but is not limited to "love, joy, peace, patience, kindness, goodness, faithfulness, gentleness and self-control. (Gal 5:22, 23 NIV)" and these are always good things.

But this is the core of Christianity – I need Saving, He does the Saving, I do the believing and we live eternally in relationship. If you have not fully bought into the Gospel on His terms then you need to reconsider everything you know and believe and even whether you actually are a Christian.

What is Common Sense?

Common Sense, as we will apply it in this case, is opening the Scriptures and finding what they have to say, not what you have heard that they say. How many times have you heard someone say something like this? "God helps those who help themselves. That's in the Bible you know." Whenever I hear this, and it happens several times a year, I reply, "I'll give you twenty bucks if you can show me that right now." I have never had to give up the money and never will, because it simply is not in the Bible. My mother used to say, "I don't like Paul. He said that women had to walk to the left and three steps behind their husbands." I challenged her to find that one too. Members of one organization of Pentecostals have told me that if you are saved you will speak in tongues.

Another fallacy of interpretation is seen in an old children's song of the Church, "Every Promise in the Book is Mine."

Every promise in the Book is mine!
Every chapter, every verse, every line.
I am standing on His Word divine,
Every promise in the Book is mine!

The implications of the song are that, as it says, every promise in the Bible belongs to every believer of the Bible. But there is a catch. As God said to Joshua

(Joshua 1:8 NIV) "Do not let this Book of the Law depart from your mouth; meditate on it day and night, so that you may be careful to do everything written in it. Then you will be prosperous and successful."

This passage was given as a personal promise to Joshua who had a specific mission given to him by God, to take the whole of the Promised Land for God's people. Unless God has called you to a similar mission then this is not your promise. And if you believe that God has called you to the same mission there may be reconsideration needed. Also, there is a caveat built into the passage where God tells Joshua to not let the book depart from his mouth, and to meditate on it day and night with a goal of doing everything written in it. Are you willing to make agreement to that caveat in your life? There is another promise given to the people of Israel in Deuteronomy that would hardly apply to everyone.

146

Deuteronomy 11:22-24 (NIV) If you carefully observe all these commands I am giving you to follow – to love the Lord your God, to walk in all his ways and to hold fast to him then the Lord will drive out all these nations before you, and you will dispossess nations larger and stronger than you. Every place where you set your foot will be yours: Your territory will extend from the desert to Lebanon, and from the Euphrates River to the western sea.

I really cannot use that as my business expansion plan. I can, however apply the idea that if I do what God commands and do all I can to walk in His ways, he will bless me. But when David is promised a descendant on the throne of Israel, is that promise mine too? Should I expect a descendant of mine on the throne? I don't think so. I have to expect the eternal reign of Christ in fulfillment of that one, and for Him to be my King, not my descendant.

And there are some things that one may take as a promise that may just be a truism, like, Proverbs 22:6 (NIV) "Train a child in the way he should go, and when he is old he will not turn from it." This is an excellent example of a truism that is mistaken for a promise. If it were in fact a promise then lots of people who did everything they thought was right would have cause to complain. But also, remember that they may have done "everything they thought was right" and still been mistaken. After all, who does a perfect job of parenting? No one! And many good people have had children that have grown up to be the opposite of good people. Still, God is the perfect parent for every one of us, and look how screwed up I am, much less you! Just kidding.

The point is to discover the proper understanding of each passage you encounter and incorporating it into a whole, instead of making it all up on your own. If we just make up our own theology then we end up with astrology, reincarnation, tarot cards, and Zoroastrianism, along with Nazism, Christian Science (which is neither Christian nor scientific), Scientology and Obamanism, to name a few. Stick to the Scriptures and try to see what God has wanted to say to you through them, instead of trying to see if you can find what you want, or passages that seem to say what you want to hear.

To do this, there are some fairly simple steps that I want you to consider.

1. Read the whole book. There are plenty of reading guides out there, but do not use a lectionary. It has its purpose, but not here.

2. You should also read it in a different version than you currently use. I recommend the NIV, NASB and the ASV as the most reliable translations available. If you are using one of those, try a different one of them.

3. When you come across a passage with which you have great familiarity and "know" what is in it, read it again, and again, change versions to avoid seeing what you "know" is there and try to see exactly what God has put there.

4. Read carefully and when in doubt of what you have read, read it again out loud.
5. Don't assume anything. Regardless of what you have been told a passage says.

Using these guidelines you may avoid some of the pitfalls that befall so many. When reading Galatians you will not see mention of a shrimp cocktail or a pork rind as many do. You won't find a way to excuse homosexuality as an acceptable choice, anymore than adultery. You won't come away thinking that you are acquitted from any sin, but forgiven on the basis of the price of the sin having been paid by Jesus. Now, grab your Bible and dig in, but **Don't Take My Word for It!**

About the Author

Keith Jenkins is the father of five wonderful children, with a sixth grandchild on the way. His greatest claim to happiness comes from being a Born-Again Believer in Jesus for his only means of Salvation. His greatest joy in life is in knowing that he and his wife, Pat, did enough things right in raising their kids that they all heard the Word of God, and became believers themselves.

Keith was an Army Brat who grew up Lutheran but also attended several other denominations before going to International Bible College and entering ministry. He was commissioned as a minister by Conrad (Connie) Walker to serve at Zion Evangelical Lutheran Church in San Antonio while in school at IBC. He has served as Parish Education leader, worship minister, and counselor to many for the past decades since. In his lifetime, Keith has worked as a McDonalds employee, barbecue helper, pizza chef, carpenter, painter's and plumber's helper, cowboy and soldier, just to mention a few. He started a computer business as a hobby over a dozen years ago and it turned into his livelihood; Computer Genius in San Antonio. With the ongoing development of his skills in finding problems and the application of information in a logical manner he has become an excellent computer and network diagnostician, but more importantly, a very reasonable, applicable, and logical Christian theologian whose motto in theology is "Don't buy the can." His actually certified genius IQ, an overall good natured sense of humor, and a voracious attachment to the Word, Keith is an excellent theologian.

Keith's wife, Patricia, is the mother of his children, has her BS in Mathematics (with a concentration in Mathematics) and MA in Multi-Disciplinary Sciences and has been a Middle School and High School teacher at the Winston School San Antonio for over a decade as of this writing. She has been a Sunday School teacher and avid student of the Word, and an excellent testimony of the patience of God in every way, especially with Keith. She is his encouragement.

Bibliography

Bibles and Scripture Tools

Logos Bible Software
http://www.logos.com/
1313 Commercial Street
Bellingham, WA 98225-4307

(ASV) The Holy Bible: American Standard Version. 1995. Oak Harbor, WA: Logos Research Systems, Inc. (electronic ed. 1901.).

(KJV) The Holy Bible: King James Version. Bellingham WA: Logos Research Systems, Inc, 1995 (electronic ed. of the 1769 edition of the 1611 Authorized Version.).

(NA27 Int.) Aland, B., Aland, K., Black, M., Martini, C. M., Metzger, B. M., & Wikgren, A. The Greek New Testament (4th ed.). Federal Republic of Germany: United Bible Societies. (1993, c1979) (electronic ed.).

(NASB) The Holy Bible: New American Standard Bible: 1995 update. LaHabra, CA: The Lockman Foundation, 1995 (electronic ed.).

(NIV) The Holy Bible: New International Version. Grand Rapids: Zondervan, 1996, c1984 (electronic ed.).

(NRSV) The Holy Bible: New Revised Standard Version. 1989. Nashville: Thomas Nelson Publishers (electronic ed.).

McReynolds, Paul R. A Greek English Inter-Linear New Testament: Carol Stream, Illinois: Tyndale House Publishing, 1992 (electronic ed.).

Encarta World English Dictionary. St. Martin´s Press/Microsoft Encarta 1999.

Endnotes

[1] *Star Wars* – 1977 – Lucasfilm Ltd. and Twentieth Century Fox

[2] *The Catholic Encyclopedia Online* –
http://www.newadvent.org/cathen/15006b.htm.

[3] Ladd, George Eldon *A Theology of the New Testament* – 1993.

[4] Morgan, Edmund S. *The Puritan Dilemma: The Story of John Winthrop* – 1958.

[5] Darwin 1871, *The Descent of Man, and Selection In Relation To Sex* pp. 200–201, Vol. 1

[6] *Jurassic Park* – 1993 http://www.imdb.com/title/tt0107290/combined

[7] *Penn & Teller: Bullshit!* – 2003 http://www.imdb.com/title/tt0672528/combined

[8] Carson, Rachel, and Lois Darling. *Silent Spring*. Boston: Houghton Mifflin ;, 1962. Print.

[9] Darwin, Charles. *The Origin of Species by Means of Natural Selection: Or, The Preservation of Favored Races in the Struggle for Life*. London: John Murray: Albemarle Street, 1859. Print.

[10] *The Terminator* – 1984 http://www.imdb.com/title/tt0088247/combined

[11] Orwell, George. *1984*. London: Secker & Warburg, 1949. Print.

[12] *Mean Girls* – 2004 http://www.imdb.com/title/tt0377092/.

[13] *King Arthur* – 2004 – Touchstone Pictures –
http://www.imdb.com/title/tt0349683/combined.

[14] *Declaration of Independence* – 1776
http://www.archives.gov/exhibits/charters/declaration.html.

[15] *Cliff Notes* – http://www.cliffsnotes.com/

[16] *Dictionary and Thesaurus – Merriam-Webster Online* - http://www.merriam-webster.com/ (www.m-w.com)

[17] N.O.W. – The National Organization of Women

[18] Murdock , George P. - *Ethnographic Atlas Codebook* – Univ of Pittsburgh Press – derived from Ethnographic Atlas recording the marital composition of 1231 societies from 1960 to 1980.

[19] Lindberg, Carter – *The European Reformations Sourcebook* – 1999 – Wiley-Blackwell Publisher. http://www.amazon.com/dp/0631213627.

[20] Kautsky, Karl – *Communism in Central Europe at the Time of the Reformation* – 1959 Russell & Russell.

[21] Fellowship of Christian Athletes – http://www.fca.org/.

[22] The Power Team – http://www.thepowerteam.com/.

[23] Discovery Channel – http://dsc.discovery.com/.

[24] Geisler, Norman L., and William E. Nix. *From God to Us: How We Got Our Bible*. Chicago: Moody, 1974. Print.

[25] Voddie Baucham – http://www.gracefamilybaptist.net/voddie-baucham-ministries

[26] Strait, George – 1998 http://www.amazon.com/dp/B000WLK8MW

[27] Pepperidge Farms® makes Goldfish®.

[28] Nabisco® (National Biscuit Company) makes Ritz® crackers.

[29] Orwell, George. *1984*. London: Secker & Warburg, 1949. Print.

[30] Dictionary.com – http://dictionary.reference.com
[31] *Will and Grace* – NBC TV – http://www.imdb.com/title/tt0157246/ .
[32] *Entourage* – HBO – http://www.imdb.com/title/tt0387199/ .
[33] *Torchwood* – BBC & Starz – http://www.imdb.com/title/tt0485301/ .
[34] *The Laramie Project* – HBO – http://www.imdb.com/title/tt0257850/ .
[35] *Happy Endings* – ABC Television – http://www.imdb.com/title/tt1587678/ .
[36] *Rent* – Chbosky, Stephen (screenplay) Larson, Jonathan (book) – http://www.imdb.com/title/tt0294870/ .
[37] *Glee* – 20th Century Fox Home Entertainment – http://www.imdb.com/title/tt1327801/ .

www.ingramcontent.com/pod-product-compliance
Lightning Source LLC
Chambersburg PA
CBHW072011040426
42447CB00009B/1581